ESSENTIAL LIFE SKILLS FOR TEENS

Build Confidence, Navigate Emotions, Foster Healthy Relationships, and Succeed in School

MARIA DAWN

Special Art

Table of Contents

Part 3 Communicating and Connecting

Part 4 Practical Living

Part 5 Personal Development

Foreword

Often described as stormy, the passage from adolescence to adulthood can be daunting, especially in the quickly changing and complex modern world in which our teens find themselves. This is why I am delighted to introduce *Essential Life Skills for Teens: Build Confidence, Navigate Emotions, Foster Healthy Relationships, and Succeed in School*. Navigating this journey with calm, and yes, enjoyment is possible for your teen (and you!) when they have essential life skills such as self-confidence, emotional regulation, healthy relationships, and academic success.

Over my three decades as a psychologist, child developmentalist, educator, and parent coach, my overarching goal has remained the same—to promote optimal outcomes for kids. I believe the most powerful way to do this is to bring research into practical application. Through the translation of key concepts into relatable, actionable guidance, this book effortlessly accomplishes this and serves as a powerful, well-considered resource to equip teens with the tools they need to thrive.

Maria Dawn achieves this by drawing on her varied and inspiring personal and professional background. She uses humor, storytelling, and deep insight to seamlessly bring together concepts and ideas with meaningful, real-life application. Honing in on what matters to teens and making frequent use of scenarios and examples, *Essential Life Skills for Teens* is engaging and relatable. It gets teens asking the important and meaningful questions and then guides them to finding answers on the path toward a successful and fulfilling future.

The book covers those key areas so critically important for not only becoming independent and achieving personal goals but doing so in a way that teens will actually enjoy the process. These essential skills include the importance of health and wellness, regulating emotions, effective communication, and developing and maintaining strong relationships. Additionally, practical advice is offered on household management, handling emergencies, financial literacy, digital best practices, and preparing for their future careers.

I applaud Maria Dawn for her skill and commitment to empowering adolescents through the pages of this authentic and comprehensive guide. I wholeheartedly recommend *Essential Life Skills for Teens* as an invaluable resource to support your teen in understanding the world around them and their place in it. As they navigate the complex, often confusing, and sometimes stormy path toward adulthood—they will have a skilled and supportive companion. And you can breathe a sigh of relief that you have some much needed assistance!

Sincerely,

Lilla Dale McManis, MEd, PhD
Psychologist and Educator

For You, the Teenager

Congrats.

You've reached the time of life when your body starts doing really strange things (like growing hair in weird places) and your emotions start flying like cannonballs. You might also feel awkward, shy, and on top of it have to deal with parents and family who currently annoy you (even if you kind of like them, too . . . even love them . . . a lot).

However, there *is* good news: you're almost an adult. And that means, you're almost old enough to get to do ANYTHING you like.

There's just one hitch: you need to be able to deal with adult life.

Like calling the dentist, fixing your car (and learning to drive one if you haven't already), cooking your own meals, doing the laundry, cleaning the house . . . the list goes on.

Not only are there those kinds of practical tasks you need to master, you also have to face what it's like making new friends, dealing with arguments, handling workmates, and so much more.

It can feel overwhelming.

In fact, most adults around age 60 or so are still getting a handle on some of the things mentioned here. Because school (unless you were really lucky) never told you how to deal with bullies on social media or what to do when your friend is being a grump.

Thankfully for you, this book will bring you a little bit of guidance. It won't hold all the answers, but hopefully it will help you—at the very least—to start asking questions so that you can find the answers.

These are some of the things you can expect to learn:

- Unlocking health and happiness (cheesy, I know, but true)
- Managing your own emotions (which is essential if you don't want to spend your life being miserable whenever things go wrong . . . and they do)
- Communicating effectively (great if you ever want a raise at work or to keep your boy/girlfriend)

- Making friends and influencing people (just like that old personal development book by Dale Carnegie claimed, there are ways and means of making a good impression)
- Building healthy relationships with the people around you (at some point, you'll realize that just because you like someone doesn't mean you'll be happy with them—that takes work)
- Learning to cope when relationships go bad (and understanding when to walk away from friends and partners who aren't treating you right)
- Conflict resolution (because everyone's a pain sometimes, including you)
- Handling emergencies (useful when someone falls and you're the only person there)
- Cleaning and householding (not only will it help you do it with flair, you will do it faster so you have more time for fun stuff unless, of course, you're a natural-born cleaner who has always enjoyed dancing with mops)
- Handling money (a.k.a. how to avoid the pitfalls that make you unable to manage basic life necessities, which is really neat if you want to have enough savings to go traveling or enjoy a night on town instead of worrying about the electricity bill and that kind of stuff)
- Preparing for the future (deciding on the path forward)
- Becoming independent (the ultimate goal)

And while I hope you'll end up reading this book glued to the page as you just can't get enough, you don't have to do that. You can dip in and out, looking up what it is you need to know.

You don't have to read about how to do your own laundry until the day you need to do it.

That said, it might be good to start reading the chapters about how to lead a healthy and happy life (it's not as boring as it sounds) and how to create great relationships. Because those things we all need to know at all times.

Above all, I hope this book will be as entertaining as it's informative and that it will give you an edge in life. An edge that will help you have more fun, hit your goals, and create incredibly amazing relationships with those around you. It might also help you understand why your parents nag about certain things.

— Maria Dawn

World traveler. Writer. Trained life coach. Actor, director, producer. Raising kids from a township in Africa. I have made many mistakes in life and learnt some of the things in this book the hard way. Others, I'm still learning. Was once a teenager with red hair and Doc Martens, who thought "My So-Called Life" would save my life, and I still think Jared Leto's voice is out of this world, but don't hold it against me.

PART 1

TAKING CHARGE OF YOU

1

Managing Your Emotions

How not to yell at your parents and siblings while slaying tests, matches, and other stressful stuff

Your siblings are annoying, your parents are having a row (that they call "an adult discussion" which only makes you more irritated because you know they're arguing and they will be happy again tomorrow—you're no longer some baby who can't handle the fact that adults argue—no big deal), and you're having a test tomorrow. You feel stressed as you need to study and frustrated by the stuff going on around you.

Now you have a choice. You can either go do something to calm yourself down and boost your mood, or you can let your stress build up until it gets so bad that it reaches a boiling point and you explode—you just can't take it anymore. That's when you'll do *anything* to relieve your stress, such as binge-watching Netflix, sitting all night complaining to your friends instead of studying, or screaming at your entire family.

You'll feel better watching Netflix than when you're trying to study but can't focus because that just makes you angrier and angrier. You'll even feel better at screaming at your family for being so loud as you're finally expressing how you feel (and you're freaking angry!). But if you do either of those things, are you in control over your emotions or are your emotions in control over you?

Will binge-watching Netflix help you study for your test? Will screaming at your family make them all calm down and stop screaming so you can study?

Probably not.

But does it have to be that way? Do you have to keep getting stressed even if there are stressful things going on around you? No. There are ways of managing your emotions.

This is true for situations like this when your entire family happens to be annoying for one night (at least in your opinion . . . and in our teens, when our hormones are flying, a lot more people sometimes seem more annoying now than they were only a year ago), but it's also true for situations that are more permanent. Some teens face losing a loved one, being lonely, having to adjust to a new life somewhere due to a sudden move, and so on.

When big things like that happen, we sometimes start feeling sad almost all the time. But there are things you can do to improve your mood, even when you're facing a difficult situation.

The hard part? When we're sad and upset, we don't *feel* like doing something to fix our mood. We have the right to be angry or sad, or whatever, because whatever is going on is going on.

Sure. You can justify what you're feeling, but does that help you?

Sometimes when you're really upset, you don't necessarily justify it; you're just too emotionally exhausted to do something.

Or are you? Don't you have just a little bit of energy to do that one little thing that will actually make you feel better?

In the next chapter, we'll look at how to destress and do things in general that keep your mood balanced, but right now let's look at what to do in the moment when things start heating up around you or you feel out of sorts in general!

Instant Mood Boosters

There are things that make you instantly happy.

Well, they won't take away all your troubles, but they change the chemicals in your mind, giving you a boost. And that boost might very well be enough for you to think clearly and make the right decisions.

Some of these things also help you focus better—almost as if they clear your mind of cobwebs.

On the flip side, some mood boosters are really bad for you if you misuse them.

For example, sugar will give you a physical rush, making you feel great (combine it with fat and you might feel even greater). But eating too much sugar will leave you feeling depleted once the rush is over, and if you eat too much sugar over a long period, it can cause inflammation in the body, leading to cancer, arthritis, and heart disease. Or it might make you gain weight or become diabetic.

That's why pleasure and discipline go hand in hand.

But there are also ways to get mood boosts that don't lead to a "crash" after the "high." Those are the kinds of mood boosts you're after. And, actually, even the right kind of sugars can work to your advantage!

Let's say you're stressed and/or feeling down. Or you simply can't focus.

You meditate for five minutes while doing a breathing exercise (i.e. it's a meditation that involves breathing so you get two for the price of one), then you go for a brisk walk or jog (or a bit of both) in nature (perhaps while listening to music that makes you genuinely happy—no sad songs, no sad lyrics), followed by a thirty-second dip in cold water in your bathtub (you can pour a bucket of hot water over yourself before getting out if you don't relish just the cold).

After the refreshing bath, you have a hot meal that contains some carbs, fat, and protein (carbs will convert to sugar, but because there's also fat and protein, chances are you won't get a sudden rush and then a crash). While eating, you watch a twenty-minute comedy show.

You finish off dinner with a square or two of dark chocolate (mood booster) and a small cup of green tea (another mood booster, but if you drink too much, you might crash), while writing down all the things in your life that are working (i.e. things that are going well—anything from the fact that you have a roof over your head to that nice compliment someone gave you).

Then you hug someone.

I can pretty much guarantee you that by the end of that, you'll feel better.

Does it sound like a lot?

If you really think about it, it isn't. Taking a few breaths to relax, then going for a walk or jog while listening to music, followed by a bath and a meal isn't really that different from a regular workout routine. And you can do it all in less than an hour.

All of the different elements in that routine are things that are known to improve mood and concentration.

Do you have to do them all at the same time? No.

Each element on its own—from going for a walk to getting a hug—can improve your mood and concentration. But if you want a big boost, try putting them all together.

Also, remember what I said about some mood boosters not being great if you misuse them? For example, while coffee can help improve your mood, drinking more than three cups a day, or simply having more than your body can tolerate in one go, can make you jittery and unfocused. And while eating when you're hungry can give you a boost, eating when you're not will only leave you lethargic.

You shouldn't leave these things to when you're feeling "down" or unfocused, either. There are things you can incorporate into your daily routine (such as exercising, meditating, and spending time in nature). Those will help balance your mood so that when stressful things happen, you don't react as strongly as you otherwise would.

In fact, in the chapter "Unlocking Health and Happiness" I talk about the things you should do consistently to ensure you're as calm and happy as possible. Because strange as it sounds, eating only junk food might be the reason why you have mood swings! As a general rule, the healthier lifestyle you have, the easier it becomes to control your emotions.

That said, we will all get upset—especially in our teens when our hormones are running amok!

And when things don't go according to your plans and you don't have an hour to do the whole routine I mentioned above? Just do what you find calms you and energizes you the most. Such as spending five minutes meditating or going for a quick walk around the block while listening to music.

It's not just about doing the above either. It's about avoiding the stuff that makes you feel bad. Such as listening to sad or aggressive music. Watching depressing movies. Looking at TikTok videos that talk about how sad someone is. Eating lots of fat and sugar. Never exercising or meditating. Never spending time outdoors. And so forth.

That's not to say you can't have a movie night while binging on a pint of ice cream. Of course you can! The important thing is to have a healthy balance. The 80/20 rule is a good guideline—stick to what's good for you 80% of the time and chances are, you'll be doing great.

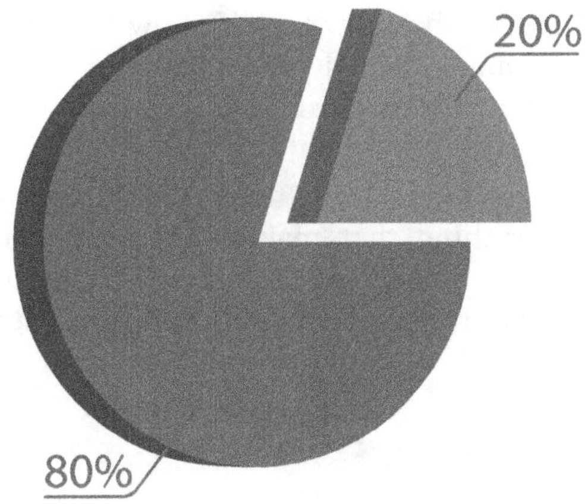

Things that can instantly improve your mood:

- Doing cardio that really gets your blood pumping (e.g. going for a run)
- Spending time in nature (greenery), particularly if you combine it with a brisk walk, swim, or jog (i.e. cardio)
- Meditating
- Doing breathing exercises
- Eating something that raises your blood sugar (but not so high it makes you crash)
- Drinking a cup of coffee (but not so much you get jittery)
- Having a quick cold bath or simply sticking your face in a bowl of cold water (don't have cold baths if you have a heart condition)
- Listening to happy or calming music (nothing sad, nothing depressing)
- Doing something that makes you laugh
- Getting a hug

- Simply shifting your focus—if you're feeling down, watching half an hour of a TV show that makes you feel good or doing an activity that distracts you from what is making you feel down can help—but you still have to face the issue (more about that later)
- Writing down everything that's working in your life right now—everything that makes you happy, that you are thankful for, and so forth—as well as things you have achieved and that can be as simple as the fact that you got out of bed and brushed your teeth this morning!

A NOTE OF WARNING

You should not do cold baths if you have heart problems—simply splash your face with cold water instead. Also, the above tips often work as they increase serotonin, dopamine, and other feel-good chemicals in the brain, but if you have *too much* of one chemical or another, some of the above tips can backfire. For example, if you have a lot of dopamine already, exercising and eating protein might make you feel wired instead of making you feel happy. You have to try things out and see what works for you.

Lastly, while I call them "happy chemicals" there's lots going on in our bodies and brains when we exercise, eat, meditate, and so forth, and that's a very simplified explanation. For example, meditation has been proven to reduce the stress hormone cortisol while increasing serotonin (a neurotransmitter) amongst other things.

Stepping Back During Tense Moments

If you're in an agitated state of mind, you say things to people that you later regret. Why? Because you're in a heightened state of mind and chances are you aren't seeing things clearly. You feel hurt, sadness, or pain, and you react to those feelings as opposed to the reality of the situation. Say your best friend stood you up, so you tell them you hate them . . . but perhaps you're just upset because lots of difficult things have been going on in your life. Now you feel alone and miserable. But you don't hate them. What you hate is how you've been feeling lately . . . and now your best friend took away that one moment of bliss you'd been looking forward to.

If you took five minutes to think it over, chances are you'd say, "I'm really sorry you can't make it. After everything that's been going on, I was looking forward to this more than you know. Can we reschedule because I really, really need something fun right now? And I'd love to see you."

While it's not your friend's responsibility to deal with your mood and what you're going through, most good friends want to be there to support you as much as they are able. In short, don't make your problems their problems, but be clear when you need some extra support!

Saying the wrong thing (or simply the first thing that pops into your mind) happens when you're excited too! Imagine you get a new job. You thank your new boss profusely, then end up babbling about how you're so short on cash you pawned your camera, snapped at your friend, can't sleep at night . . . and so on. It might take you a full few minutes before you realize what you're doing. And your boss is, perhaps, not the best person to talk to about your financial difficulties. At least not until you get to know them properly!

Of course, not everyone reacts the same way. Perhaps, you throw your arms around your new boss and kiss them on the cheek instead of shaking their hand as you intended to. Or you tell them that hiring you is the best thing they've ever done because you're going to make them a billionaire. While both enthusiasm and confidence are great, being overly enthusiastic or confident can be misinterpreted. And chances are you don't really think you'll make your new boss a billionaire. You're just so happy that you end up exaggerating.

Look, obviously, you'll have to learn to control yourself when things like these happen and you need to respond on the spot and face-to-face, but if you get super excited when you receive an email, don't respond right away. Wait. Take some deep breaths. Go make a cup of tea. Watch a movie. Wait until you feel your mood has changed a bit. Then you can re-read the email to check that you didn't misinterpret something and go ahead and write a clear-headed reply.

The truth is, getting overly upset or happy usually doesn't help us, which leads us to the next point: balance.

Balancing the Good with the Bad: A Healthy Approach to Life

As you grow older, you learn that life is filled with good and bad.

If something bad happens, you know that eventually things will change.

If something good happens, you know that eventually things will change.

That prevents you from getting super upset by the bad and over-the-top excited about the good.

But you want to be excited, right?

Sure, but if it gets too much, it's followed by a crash. It's nice to be happy. To feel good. But not to be so excited you get jittery and then feel awful once the "high" is over.

The instant mood boosters can also help calm you down and improve your mood when something not so pleasant happens. Instead of sitting and thinking about how bad your test went, meditate and breathe for five minutes, go for a run, have a cold bath (or at least stick your head in some cold water), and eat a nice meal while chatting to a positive friend or watching some comedy. After that, chances are you won't feel all that bad about the test. And if your calendar is filled with activities you love, goals to accomplish, and social events, you won't have time to sit pondering how your life will go downhill because of this one bad test.

Let's make an example. Marcus (who happens to be one of your absolute favorite people in the world and whom you haven't seen for months) tells you he'll take you ice skating next weekend. You get super excited. All you can think about is ice skating. You daydream about it so much that you don't pay attention to school, you say no to hanging out with friends as you want to prep for the ice skating, and you cancel on the birthday party you were supposed to attend that Saturday instead of telling Marcus you can't go.

Now, let's say Marcus ends up breaking his leg when skiing (or, more likely, gets a cold) and cancels your ice skating. Not only are you disappointed you don't get to skate with Marcus, you've also canceled on the birthday party, got a D on an essay (which you now have to rewrite), and have to do all the math homework that you skipped during the week.

If you'd decided to go skating with Marcus on the Sunday instead and paid attention during the week, you wouldn't be behind in schoolwork, you'd still be going to the party, and you wouldn't feel like the world came to an abrupt end when Marcus canceled.

Another time, you might get so excited about a new job that you spend all your time working and trying to prove yourself. By doing so, you stop going to the gym, stop hanging out with friends, and neglect your relationship. When the company goes bust, you're left without a job and with a bad relationship and bad social life.

You should invest in projects and people. You should allow yourself to be happy when something good happens. You just have to make sure you don't place all you've got on one thing and then feel terrible when that one thing does not pan out.

Let's say you want to go to Yale University. Only, you're not accepted. You're certain the universities you were accepted to, like Berkeley, just won't compare. But one visit to campus and you're in love.

Or you spend all your time at Berkeley sulking that you're not at Yale and fail to see all the opportunities right in front of you to have fun and excel academically.

Actually, I had a situation a bit like that. I wanted to go to NYU and was accepted (TISCH School of the Arts) and I was gutted when I couldn't figure out a way to pay the fees. It was my dream. Instead, I was stuck in drama school in London.

I can safely say that the drama school I attended in London turned me into a very good director. What's more, years later when I decided I was going to study in the US, I ended up at UCLA in LA. That was the one city I thought I'd hate and the one school I was intent on not attending. Only I fell madly in love with it. The thought of living in New York after I discovered LA, well, it just didn't compare.

Just because a door is closed doesn't mean something bad just happened. It feels that way, sure, but there are so many other things that could happen that are *better*. Remember that the next time you have a breakup, fall out with a friend, don't get accepted to a school, program, or job, or your plans are suddenly canceled. There are a million possibilities, and you might just have been set free to pursue your true dreams.

Sometimes things truly are bad. If someone passes away, you lose a lot of money, you have to temporarily live in a place you loathe due to circumstances . . . there are many things in life that can be difficult. That's not to say there won't be other things that are good, even great. So no matter how hard the situation is, don't blind yourself to the good out there. Keep believing in it and reaching for it as then you're more likely to find it.

How many yellow cars did you see yesterday? Chances are you won't know because you weren't looking for yellow cars. But if you open your eyes to yellow cars, you will see them. Just as you'll see good things when they come your way and the opportunities that exist all around us.

TIPS If you get upset or over-the-top excited, sit down and do a breathing exercise for five minutes or revisit one of the other mood boosters mentioned in this book.

Who Rules Over Your Thoughts? You Do!

My principal in drama school, Sam Kogan, said of the mind, "It takes control over you, until you take control over it." I believe he was right.

Do you remember what you were thinking about when you last tied your shoelaces? Probably not. But you were thinking of something. Chances are you can't even remember what you were thinking five minutes ago. The interesting part is we tend to think things we aren't even aware of.

Let's say it's a normal day, you wake up, shower, have breakfast, then you notice you're feeling down. Why?

You don't know until you start asking yourself what you've been thinking about.

In between showering, making breakfast, eating it, and texting your friends while eating, you worry about getting into a specific college, how well you did at the last math exam, and if your dog is getting older and going to die soon (as you fed him and he looked . . . old).

This is why it's so important to start to notice our thoughts and take charge of them. Especially when something upsets us, but even in day-to-day life.

If you start thinking about everything that could go wrong or has gone wrong, or how awful you are, or something of that sort, stop. Ask yourself why you're thinking them. And if there's an emotion you need to face, face it. Then do something that forces you to think about something else. Listen to an audiobook. Watch a movie. Go for a run while listening to an audiobook or some happy music. Distract yourself.

While you have to face your emotions (if someone has just died, you failed an exam, you lost a job or a friend, whatever it might be, you need to face your feelings around it), you can't wallow in them. At least not the negative ones. Face them, then let them go.

What do I mean by facing your emotions? Take three to five minutes when you sit down and feel into them. Feel what it's like to be disappointed about your failed exam or lose a friend. Really feel it. Then let it go. Ask yourself what would be the most productive step forward.

If you've just lost a friend and feel lonely, what can you do to feel loved and make more friends?

If you've failed a test and are fretting about not getting into med school anymore, what can you do to assure you get into med school? Study? Apply for a job for summer? Do some extracurricular activities? Work on your college application? Ask your teacher for a chance to improve your grades by doing some extra assignments or retaking the test?

And here's something you'll want to remember: when stressed, we sometimes automatically do things to distract ourselves, but they aren't necessarily good for us.

We're stressed about an upcoming test. Instead of sitting down and facing the stress, then doing something like meditating for ten minutes to calm ourselves before studying, we procrastinate.

We can't handle our own stress levels, so we use coping mechanisms.

Those coping mechanisms range from eating too much chocolate to binge-watching Netflix—when you do those things you forget about your stress. We all have different coping mechanisms. Some people work out too much; others drink too much.

As mentioned in the part about mood boosters, there are things you can do to raise your mood—things that are pleasurable and raise your spirits—but even those need to be done in moderation.

A piece or two of dark chocolate after a meal, while sipping a small cup of green tea, can boost your mood. Eating three bars of sugary chocolate during the day while drinking five cups of coffee is not going to help you. It's going to harm you. It won't boost your mood; it will tank your mood.

Even things like exercise and meditation can be done to excess—a fifteen-to twenty-minute run followed by stretching and breathing exercises, a quick shower, and a meal can help you focus. Going for a one-hour jog, followed by a twenty-minute bath, and a one-hour meal is going to waste your time if you need to study. It's not going to harm your health, but it's not going to help you face what you need to do: studying. You can go for a one-hour jog on the weekend instead.

If something bothers you—school, your parents, your siblings, your friends, your charity work, your coach . . . whatever it might be—you have to face the problem.

You can do something to manage your emotions (such as meditating and exercising) to help you face it, but you have to sit down and look at what the issue is and how to overcome it. If you have a problem with the soccer coach, who else can help advise you on how to deal with it? Who is great with people and problem-solving whom you feel comfortable talking with and who would do so in confidence?

What I'm trying to say is that if something bad happens or something simply irritates you or you have a problem with, face your emotions around it. Take five minutes to sit with the feeling.

Then do something to feel better, such as meditating or exercising.

Then tackle the problem—what can I do to handle this?

If you need it after that, do something else to boost your mood, such as a set time watching comedy (let's say, twenty minutes).

Then move on to other areas of your life.

> Do not wallow in the thoughts and feelings around what upsets you or is a problem area of your life.

Do not go to extremes to lose yourself from the problem or the feelings around you (such as spending all your money going on a shopping spree, playing some game from morning till night, sticking your head in books every waking minute, binge-watching Netflix, drinking or getting high, binge-eating unhealthy foods, or anything else that helps you cope but isn't good for you).

That said, as mentioned earlier in this section, if you're feeling particularly blue one day, after you've faced your thoughts (and asked why you're thinking thoughts that are making you feel that way), you can do things to have fun and distract yourself. You need to keep building "happy chemicals" if you have a tendency to walk down the "dark" paths in your mind—thinking thoughts that are not helping you.

What I'm trying to establish is that there has to be balance—you can't always spend the entire day doing "happy things." That will only lead to destruction if there are other things that need to get done. But if you find that in your spare time you tend to get depressed, then face your thoughts and emotions, use a natural mood booster, and after that, engage in something that raises your spirits. Find somewhere to volunteer. Call a friend. Watch a good movie with an uplifting message. Go to the theater (if you're lucky enough to even have a theater with something good where you live . . . I trained in theater so I just have to sneak it in here!). Play sports. Go for a hike with friends.

Here are some things to ask yourself:

- Am I berating myself for my mistakes or seeing what I've done well?
- Am I looking at what I can't do or what I can do?
- Am I staring at the problem or looking for solutions?
- Am I thinking about the bad things in life or the good things in life?
- Am I thinking about sad or happy memories?

In short, where's your focus? Shift it and your life will shift with it.

Rethinking Your Reactions

You know your mom gets upset every time you fail a test. This is because she's anxious and fretting about you doing well in life and school has never really been your thing—you're more athletic, good with your hands, or artistic. Even if you know you won't pursue a career in academics (at least you don't think so . . . Einstein got kicked out of school after all, so perhaps you'll change your mind one day), you still want to know that it will serve you to do decently well in school, as it'll help you through some aspects of life. While you're working to improve your grades, you know there will still be times where you fail a test. You also know that your mother isn't going to change, no matter how much you'd prefer that she praised your progress instead of moaning about your hiccups.

When this happens, perhaps you get angry with your mom. Because seriously, it's unfair. Perhaps you aren't prone to anger but instead tend to walk away. Shutting her out. Problem being, when she next comes to show you love, you might shut that out, too.

You'd like to respond to your mom and say, "Look, Mom, I know you're upset as you want me to do well. You also feel you work hard for me, so you want me to work hard for myself, so I can have a good future. I get it. But I want you to know that I *am* working hard. I *am* improving. And I'd really like it if you could acknowledge that. So I feel good. And try even more. Now, I just feel defeated. I've put in all this time, and I'm still not nailing it. Why keep trying? But I know *why* I should keep trying. I just need to feel . . . happy. Inspired. That will help me to get through it. Do you think we can work on this together?"

So how do you change your response? Well, you imagine it.

You sit down and imagine your mother saying what she says when she's upset and how it makes you feel. You imagine taking a breath and calming yourself down. Telling yourself your mother is only upset because she wants you to succeed. She's showing it in the wrong way, but actually, she loves you. It's just not the way *you* need to be loved to feel inspired to work harder. She might think tough love will do it, but it's not doing it.

Right. So that will help you feel better. Then you practice, in your mind, to tell her what you want to tell her.

You do this exercise a couple of times—maybe three or four. Enough times till it feels natural to react *as you want to react.*

An exercise I talk about in later chapters is doing this kind of imagining every morning and every night. In the morning, you imagine how you want the day to go and work on how you want to react to different things.

At night, you think through how the day went, then rethink it as you would have wanted to react in various situations (if you didn't react the way you wanted to).

By doing this, we rewire our brains. We take charge of who we want to be in different situations. It was first taught to me by my drama school principal, but you will find it in *Psycho-Cybernetics*, too, where it's referred to as "shadow boxing."

Remember to take a few breaths and relax your body before you start imagining.

Can you see how you can do this before a soccer game? A social event you dread? An upcoming talk with someone? Doing a presentation?

Think of it as an actor preparing for a role—you imagine who you want to be. Acknowledge any feelings that come up—such as the nervousness you will likely feel when stepping on stage for a big role. Then choose to think and feel what you'd like to think and feel in that instance. "I'm here to do a role I know well. I'm here to entertain the audience—to give them joy. I'm going to let go and step into my role." Then feel yourself being on stage acting and how good it feels to be the character.

Self-Esteem: The Power of YOU

Self-esteem is simple.

Think about all the things you achieved today. And yes, getting out of bed was one of them.

Think about all the things you've learned in your life so far.

Think about all the things that went totally wrong but that you can now revisit and learn from. Turn your heartache into something to be grateful for. You went down. You got up. Now you're happy just to be standing and having learned what you did.

Think about all the good qualities you have.

Think about the people whom you've made smile.

Think about every kind action you've ever performed. And yes, putting down the toilet seat counts, though I'm not sure the men in your family will be thanking you. But seriously, closing the lid of a toilet is a kind gesture, isn't it?

Consider the fact that you're just a human like all other humans. Neither more, nor less. You have some experiences and an innate biology which shape you. You do your best to overcome your flaws. You do your best to treat yourself, people, and the planet with respect. That's it. You're perfect just doing that. Just being.

If, on the other hand, you think about everything that went wrong today. Everything that went wrong yesterday. And everything that might go wrong in the future. Well, chances are you're beating yourself up, berating yourself, and not seeing the value you add.

Likewise, if you belittle things, it doesn't work. "Sure, the physics teacher is always nice to me, but they're just a teacher. No one important." Actually, they are as important as every other person on this planet.

You're stuck with bullies at school, at home, or somewhere else. But do you also have people who value you? Even if it's just the English teacher who thanked you for doing well in class. Or the shopkeeper who gets happy every time you smile at them. Then, you're making life better for someone. Focus on that.

And focus on all you've accomplished—it might not seem much now, but you learned to walk. Talk. Read. Speak. Or perhaps not if you're blind, deaf, or speech impaired. But you learned something, or you wouldn't have been reading or listening to this right now. You did well. Especially if you had or are having difficulties and are still reading this.

You're beautiful because you're a human soul who experiences joy, sadness, loss, happiness, love . . . that takes bravery. And that alone makes you beautiful.

And even if you haven't experienced it yet, even if your life until now has been hard and filled with arguments and difficult people, you will one day make someone smile. You can try today by smiling at the next person you see.

You don't have to achieve a ton of things to be worthy of love, kindness, or anything else. You're human. That's enough.

Now, focus on all the good in your life. The good you do. The good you have done. The fact that you're brave enough to get up in the morning and peek outside your covers.

That makes you freakin' fantastic.

2

Unlocking Health and Happiness

How to become happier and live longer

Growing up I always thought there were two things to maintain good health: diet and exercise. Everyone kept blabbering on about how one should exercise tons and cut fat (and later discovered that wasn't so good if you cut it *all*).

Then, I started taking an interest in health and well-being. I almost became a doctor but ended up writing articles about health instead. And discovered that things like sleep affect your immune system and mood. Spending time in nature can improve your mood and boost your immune system. Stress can cut years off your life as it causes disease. Meditation can reduce stress. Socializing can make you live longer . . . seriously, it improves longevity according to some studies.

So it's not all about diet and exercise—though they do play a big role in our health and well-being.

Interestingly, what makes you healthy also tends to make you happy and what makes you happy tends to make you healthy.

You might be rolling your eyes, already thinking exercise and healthy diets are boring. And isn't it obvious what makes us happy? Having fun with friends and doing stuff we enjoy.

The thing is, most of us go through periods in life that are difficult. It could be in our teens, or it could be later. But if we establish habits that keep us healthy and help release "happy chemicals" in our brain, it's easier to get through those periods. Our mood is better, we have higher energy levels, and we're less likely to do things like binge-eating pizza or getting drunk to try to cope with the difficulties. We are also more likely to deal with breakups better as we aren't relying on other people to make us happy.

Plus, I promise you don't have to eat lots of boring foods or get a gym membership to be able to eat well and exercise! And don't worry—even if there's a lot of information in this chapter, there's an excellent cheat sheet in the end that makes it all very simple! But that cheat sheet only makes sense if you read the whole chapter first.

Nourishing Your Body—the Basics of a Healthy Diet

First of all, let's start by saying I'm not a dietician, nor a doctor. The best thing when changing your diet is to see a specialist as your body is unique. I can only tell you about what is, generally speaking, considered healthy. And give you some tips for fun foods to eat that are actually both healthy and tasty!

The right diet can help improve your health, mood, and longevity. In fact, if you don't eat right, you can become sick, depressed, or lethargic. You can also experience mood swings, an inability to focus, and other negative symptoms.

Unfortunately, you can't have a blood test that shows you are 5% less energetic than you could be and 10% more grumpy because you're eating the wrong foods. All we know is that we need *the right* food to function properly.

But there are so many diets today, so which one to follow?

Well, that's debatable. But when I started taking a serious interest in this and googled where in the world people lived the longest, I discovered two things.

Monaco, as a country, had people with the longest life spans. Most people in Monaco are wealthy, so it stands to reason they have the money to eat well and get good healthcare.

The second thing I discovered was that there are so-called Blue Zones around the world where people live the longest.

In these Blue Zones, people eat foods similar to the Mediterranean diet.That means they eat a lot of veggies (including leafy greens and cruciferous vegetables), whole grains, pulses (about half a cup of beans daily!), fruits, berries, and nuts. They also eat small amounts of oil, fish, dairy, eggs, and meat (some eat no meat at all).

What they consume very little of are preservatives, processed meats, coloring agents, hydrogenated oils, super refined sugars such as glucose syrup, and anything else that isn't strictly natural.

In short, people living in the Blue Zones cook their meals from scratch using fresh, mainly organic and wholemeal, ingredients.

Now, I'm not here to tell you that that's how you *have* to eat. But while the debate might still be raging among professionals whether you should or should not eat gluten, whether paleo is better than vegan, and so forth, one thing they all seem to agree on is this: eat fresh whole foods and lots of vegetables and avoid processed and prepackaged foods as much as possible.

In other words, a whole foods diet or a diet consisting of "clean" (i.e. unprocessed) foods appears to be what everyone agrees on which makes sense—you eat the foods nature provided us with.

It also appears that some herbs and spices can be good for you, granted you don't overdo it (as some are potent). So add them to your meals to make them more flavorful and try drinking herbal teas. Which brings us to the next point: it's not just what you eat, but also what you drink.

The best thing you can drink is pure water (i.e. spring water) or herbal tea (so long as you vary the herbs and check with a professional that there aren't some you should avoid—licorice can, for example, affect your blood pressure). You can also do flavored water by sticking cucumber and mint, or whatever flavor you prefer, into a pitcher and letting it sit for a while— some people like to add berries, or lemon balm, for example, while others like a slice of lemon or lime.

There are other drinks that come with health benefits too but you can only drink in moderation or they become unhealthy, such as coffee, caffeinated teas, raw juice, kombucha, and red wine (once you're old enough to drink it). I'm personally fairly sure that hot chocolate made with nut milk, cacao, and honey can, in small amounts, also be good for you. Cacao is filled with antioxidants, honey has healing properties, and nut milk, well, it's made with nuts which are good for you. So it's a nice and fairly healthy treat!

Bear in mind that those drinks are only good in moderation. Raw juice, for example, is filled with antioxidants and nutrients, but it's also filled with sugar if it's made with fruit. Red wine contains resveratrol (a powerful antioxidant), but it also contains alcohol which can badly damage your body.

One last thing to remember is that you need different types of foods.

You need fat:

> Oils, butter, avocados, dairy, fatty meat, fatty fish, nuts

You need **protein**:

> Lentils, beans, nuts, peanuts which aren't really nuts, almonds, quinoa, soybeans and therefore tofu, fish, eggs, dairy, and meat

You need carbs:

> Fruits, berries, vegetables, grains, beans, lentils, and peanuts

You need fiber:

> Beans, lentils, vegetables, fruits, nuts, and wholemeal grains

All of the above also contain vitamins and various other nifty things, like antioxidants that help fight free radicals (mainly found in fruits, veggies, tea, coffee, wine, and cacao, i.e. anything coming from plants). And by eating a varied diet rich in vegetables, fruits, pulses, and berries, with smaller amounts of wholemeal grains, nuts, oils, fish, meat, eggs, and dairy, you tend to get what you need from your diet.

Consider this: you can eat a ton of different veggies providing the same amount of calories a fairly small chunk of white bread would. However, the veggies would provide *a lot* of different nutrients, while the white bread wouldn't.

You want to eat a nutrient-rich diet but also allow yourself a slice of bread if that makes you happy.

Now, you know what foods and drinks are, generally speaking, considered good . . . but how do you go about changing your diet? If you're used to eating certain foods, it can feel overwhelming to suddenly change everything around.

How do you get around that?

You change one thing at a time. That way, it becomes very easy.

Below are some suggestions for how to change your diet bit by bit if needed—perhaps you're already eating a great diet! You don't have to do it in this order, just choose one thing per week to tackle.

Week One: Drinking Right

If you're drinking lots of milk, soda, juice, and coffee, switch to drinking mainly water and herbal tea. You can still drink the other drinks, just in smaller amounts.

If you normally drink three sodas a day, going cold turkey and drinking none at all might be a bit harsh as you're used to your "sugar rushes." It can feel really hard to give up on the rush you feel after having a lot of sugar. So, instead of torturing yourself and drinking only water, swap the sodas one by one to raw juice and then to water or herbal tea (day one, you have one raw juice and two sodas; day two, two raw juices and one soda; day three, only raw juices; day four, one glass of water and two raw juices; and day five, one raw juice and two glasses of water, which is a pretty nice balance).

If you're used to drinking caffeinated sodas, you might want to swap them for tea sweetened with honey at first, so that you still get a bit of caffeine and sugar but not as much as you would if downing the sodas. Then, gradually cut down.

Of course, you can still drink sodas, but keep it as a treat rather than something you do every day.

Week Two: Swapping Sugar for Healthier Alternatives

Swap sugar for a healthier sweetener whenever possible. If you use sugar in your coffee, swap it with honey (and gradually cut down on the amount if you use a lot). If you cook with sugar, swap it with stevia, honey, maple syrup, agave syrup, or date syrup. You can also try using some coconut sugar and brown sugar instead of white sugar when baking.

Sometimes you might need to mix and match. For example, when baking, you might want to swap some of the sugar in the recipe for stevia. But you can't get rid of all of the sugar as it would change the consistency of the cake. What's more, stevia has a funny aftertaste. I love it when making gingerbread cake, but it's horrible when taken in coffee or when combined with chocolate (in my opinion).

If you tend to buy a lot of sugary treats, try to swap them with something healthier, too. Here are some examples:

Doughnut	baked apple with cinnamon and honey or maple syrup
Candy	dried fruit or pieces of fruit or frozen fruit (mango, grapes, blueberries)
Sweetened yogurt	yogurt with berries and honey—after a while, you might want to get rid of the honey, too
Ice cream	(vegan) ice cream sweetened with erythritol or maple syrup, frozen smoothie popsicles, or frozen raw juice popsicles, frozen bananas covered in peanut butter and dark chocolate
Sorbet	frozen berries with avo and a touch of honey or maple syrup blended together to create a sorbet-like consistency (a strong blender is best for this purpose, but one can make do with a regular blender, the consistency just isn't as smooth, however)
Chocolate mousse	blend avo, cacao, and honey with a splash of vegan milk to make a vegan version that's healthier (might sound horrible, tastes divine)
Strawberry mousse	strawberry chia seed pudding made with coconut milk and sweetened with honey

Eventually, try to cut down on foods with sugar, but phase it out. You can even keep a diary for it. And if you google it, you'll find plenty of ideas for healthy treats so you won't be deprived of fun foods!

Week Three: Tackling Snacks

If you tend to snack on unhealthy things, try to prep snacks that are good for you that you can bring along in your bag. Below are some ideas for pretty healthy snacks:

- Raw and/or dry roasted nuts
- Apple slices (and carrot sticks if you like) with peanut butter

- Fruit salad (though not too big and note that your blood sugar might drop a while later, depending on what you put into the salad, so have something else ready if that happens)
- A boiled egg
- Crudites (raw veggies) to dip in hummus (or a white bean dip), guacamole (or other avo dip), baba ganoush, or some other dip you like—even crème fraiche with some spice mix
- Homemade popcorn instead of crisps
- Baked potato wedges instead of french fries
- Healthy cookies like oatmeal cookies (if you're prone to snacking on more sugary ones)
- Protein smoothies (don't overdo the amount of fruit in there, and remember, you don't need protein powder, you can add nut butters to get protein, too)
- A small wholemeal sandwich or some crisp bread with almond butter
- Roasted chickpeas

This should give you some ideas, but a quick look on Google or Pinterest will help you find a ton of healthy snacks (or at least *healthier* snacks than crisps and chocolate cookies).

Again, if you feel overwhelmed, you don't have to swap *all* your snacks at *once*. If you have snacks three times a day, start with swapping your first snack of the day for something healthier. Get used to that. Three days later, look into swapping the second one.

Week Four: Cut Down on Dairy

By all means, have dairy (unless you're intolerant or allergic), but don't have *too much*. If you love big lattes, try using a vegan milk, like a nut milk or oat milk instead. Not creamy enough? Get a vegan creamer (without strange additives) and add a little bit OR use a splash of real cream. I tend to add a little bit of real cream to my vegan milk when making coffee.

There's no reason you should stop eating cheese, especially hard cheese, as it contains very little lactose (what most people are intolerant to), but stay away from processed cheese, and if you mainly have cheese on bread, try some other toppings, like almond butter, or hummus, a couple of times a week.

NOTE

You don't want to buy vegan milks filled with funny additives. Find a good brand or make your own nut or oat milk. Drinking lots of soy milk might not be good for you either, so just as with regular milk, cut down. You don't have to stop drinking neither regular milk nor soy milk, just beware not to have too much of it.

Week Five: Have a Healthy Breakfast

If you're currently eating sugary cereal or white toast for breakfast, try changing to something more healthy. Here are some ideas:

- A green smoothie followed by a wholemeal sandwich an hour or so later (if it's a protein smoothie, you might not need the sandwich)
- Oatmeal porridge with honey, nuts, and seeds or some nice jam (if you add some coconut cream, it gets really nice and creamy and is actually very nice cold, almost like a pudding)
- Overnight oats
- Chia seed and coconut cream pudding (as a treat)
- Yogurt with some fruit followed by a boiled egg and a wholemeal toast an hour or so later
- Half a grapefruit followed by yogurt with a wholemeal cereal (one that isn't too sugary!)

Pinterest is a goldmine when looking for cool recipes to try, so just type in "healthy breakfast" and you'll find tons of ideas for what to make.

Week Six: Go Wholemeal

There seems to be a consensus that you should try to eat a variety of different grains, not just wheat, and that you should stick to wholemeal grains. That means you choose brown rice instead of white rice, brown bread instead of white bread, wholemeal pasta instead of white pasta, and so forth. These days there are also funky alternatives like pasta made with lentils and beans.

It's also good to mix things up so you get different nutrients. If you're always eating bread for lunch, try rice cakes. If you love your rice, try swapping it for quinoa sometimes.

This is not to say you should never have white rice or pasta or enjoy a fluffy white bread. It's just important that you get different nutrients and try to eat as many wholemeal grains as possible. So if you have the option to choose what kind of bread, pasta, or rice you eat, make sure that you mainly choose wholemeal.

On weeks seven and eight, you can focus on creating healthy lunches and dinners. I'm not going to give you recipes for those—it depends on what you enjoy eating and whether you eat meat or not.

That said, a good place to start is to look at what you buy that's processed and swap it for something less processed. For example, if you buy a lot of burgers, swap the processed ones for proper beef, chicken, turkey, or ostrich burgers that don't have any additives. Or make your own from minced meat.

And if you're looking for a healthy lunch, try either a soup/broth or salad with a wholemeal sandwich. Both salads and soups are packed full of nutrients (granted they contain wholemeal ingredients). You can also add green smoothies and juices to your diet to increase your nutrient intake.

Another tip to make a meal healthier is to start with a salad and then have a smaller amount of whatever you'd normally eat (if what you normally eat isn't too healthy).

This brings us to the 80/20 rule. Eat 80% according to your diet, but feel free to pig out on some things. There's nothing wrong with eating a burger a week. There's everything wrong with eating a burger a day. There's nothing wrong with having dessert, so long as it's a tiny dessert after lunch or dinner and not a massive one after every meal.

Schedule your treats. If you love milkshakes, congratulate yourself on a Friday after the school week is done by having one. If you adore pie, make it a tradition to bake pies on a Sunday. Just make sure you don't find excuses to have massive treats every day.

Also, if you know you love something sweet with your coffee or after a meal, make sure to pack some healthy treats in your bag, such as some squares of dark chocolate or some healthy biscuits. That way, you know you won't be buying a giant muffin or some super unhealthy chocolate bar but you will still get a treat. And that's important—you deserve to eat stuff you love.

I'm a big believer in loving what you eat—if you try to follow some horrid diet that makes you miserable, what's the point? You need to be able to enjoy your food. That said, I know that once you change what you eat, your taste buds change. If you eat only salad for a week, by the time you start eating regular food again, I bet that any unnatural flavoring will taste really weird. You'll need less salt to make something taste salty, too.

What I'm trying to say is that once your taste buds adjust, you're going to love eating a healthy diet. You just have to have some patience and ensure you find foods you enjoy.

Consider this your cheat sheet.

- Cut down on processed foods (processed meat such as smoked ham, refined sugar, refined grains such as white rice and flour, hydrogenated oils, and prepackaged foods containing unnatural additives)
- Eat lots of whole foods, such as vegetables (including leafy greens and cruciferous vegetables), fruits, berries, wholemeal grains, pulses, and nuts
- Eat small amounts of meat, dairy, eggs, spices, herbs, and oils
- Stick with the 80/20 rule—eat healthy at least 80% of the time
- When changing your diet, do it bit by bit—swap unhealthy drinks, snacks, breakfast, lunch, dinner, and dessert to healthy ones (you can tackle one per week, for example)

NOTE

Always speak with a professional about what diet works best for you. Your body is unique. People break down food differently. People are more or less physically active. People might take medications that don't go well with certain foods, spices, or herbs.

Sweat It!

This is easy. Really. You don't have to get a fitness instructor (but it helps as they can give you exercises to keep ALL your muscles trim and support your body correctly). You don't need to sign up to a gym. You don't have to do yoga. You don't even have to like to exercise.

Here's the deal. You want to stretch. You want to get some nice cardio in (anything that gets your pulse racing). You want to get some strength exercises in.

All it takes is twenty minutes a day. Run like the wind or power walk for fifteen minutes, stretch for five. Dance around your living room like it was 1970 and you owned the dance floor for fifteen minutes. Stretch for five.

Vacuum the floor, while stopping every so often to do some jumping. Finish with a good stretch.

Do push-ups for five minutes, sit-ups for five minutes, and leg work for five minutes. Finish with stretching for five. YouTube will tell you how to do arm, leg, and core muscle building if you don't know, or you can hire a personal trainer to give you a 15–30 minute program to work on at home, with or without weights.

Alternatively, you do legs one day, arms one day, and core one day.

Start your day with twenty sun salutations or other yoga poses that you can perform fast enough to get your pulse racing followed by ten minutes of stretching.

Walk for thirty seconds. Run (or jump) for ten. Walk for three minutes, run (or jump) for one. Keep going at whatever intervals you like for at least fifteen minutes.

The important thing? Exercise for fifteen to sixty minutes per day. Would twenty to thirty minutes be better than fifteen minutes? Probably, but fifteen minutes, followed by five minutes worth of stretching is the minimum goal. Cardio is super important, so you want to incorporate that more often than not.

Once a week, do a longer stretching program if you're only stretching for five minutes the other days of the week.

If you prefer going to the gym, doing ballet, playing soccer, or what have you, then do that at least three times per week (assuming each session is at least sixty minutes long). If you can, add ten minutes of exercise the other days of the week.

In short, move your butt, while also ensuring you work your muscles. And if you aren't an exercise fan, don't overcomplicate it. Simply commit to moving about for fifteen minutes per day—twenty or thirty if you can.

Destressing

Stress causes disease because it causes inflammation in your body, among other things. As a result, it's really important to destress.

How do you destress?

Perhaps by walking. Dancing. Cooking. Building with Lego. Cleaning (yes, truly, it works for some). Painting. Boxing. A hot bath. Meditation.

Take your pick. Whatever makes you feel truly zen.

While talking about destressing, it helps not to get stressed in the first place. If something in your life is bothering you, stop for long enough to deal with it. Figure it out.

Most importantly, spend some time every day to destress. Not in front of the television or your phone. Do something that relaxes you—be it knitting, meditating, fixing up a car, drawing, baking, walking (then you get your cardio in, too), or singing.

Go Zen—Meditation and Breathing Exercises

I guess this could count as part of destressing, but truly, you should find things to do that makes you feel relaxed *and* meditate *and* do breathing exercise (don't worry—it only takes five minutes!). These are different forms of relaxation.

Let's start with meditation. Why should you join the yogis and new agers and start meditating? Because time sand time again, studies have found that meditation improves your cognitive (brain) functioning and reduces your stress levels, which in turn improves your health. It can also help improve your mood.

In short, if you want to stay happy and healthy and make sure your brain is razor sharp, you should start meditating.

If meditation sounds like some sort of woo-woo practice to you, don't worry. It's simply about relaxing your mind and body.

These days, there are a ton of guided meditations available on YouTube and a gazillion meditation apps for Android and iOS. If you like guided meditation, this is the way to go.

If you just want to meditate on your own, a good way to start is to first relax your body.

Close your eyes. Slowly breathe in and out through your nose, or in through your nose and out through your mouth. Then start feeling into each body part, saying (in your mind, not out loud), "I'm relaxing my toes, my toes are completely relaxed." And so forth, going through all body parts and organs (so your kidneys, pancreas, heart, lungs, and so forth) until you reach the top of your head. When you get there, say, "I'm relaxing my body and mind, my body and mind are completely relaxed."

Then you can stay in that relaxed state of mind for a while, while focusing on your breathing. Or you can move on to some other form of meditation.

Breathing also forms part of many meditation exercises.

We all breathe, but the interesting thing is that doing breathing exercises for five minutes can change your brain chemistry.

Yup.

Feeling down in the dumps? Can't concentrate on schoolwork? Feeling upset? Feeling frustrated? Try doing breathing exercises for five minutes and see what happens.

As with meditation, there are plenty of breathing exercises to be found online—both on platforms like YouTube and TikTok, as well as through blogs, magazines, and apps.

If you just want to try it out without spending time online, breathe in slowly through your nose. Hold for a count of eight (or more if you can). Breathe out through your mouth—but slowly. Perhaps shape your mouth as if you were blowing (like an "O," in other words). Hold for a count of eight. Then start over and repeat. Do this for five minutes.

The first few times you do it, have an adult with you in the room in case you feel dizzy or faint. If you do, stop.

See how you feel before and after doing it.

NOTE

If you suffer from low blood pressure or any other condition that makes you prone to fainting, or have a condition affecting your heart or lungs, consult with a doctor about doing breathing exercises. If you suffer from asthma, there are specific breathing exercises you can look for that might help you.

Embracing the Great Outdoors

No, you don't have to become a scout or go camping (unless you really want to). What you should do, on the other hand, is make sure to spend some time in nature (or at the very least: outdoors) every day, or if you can't, head for a hike on the weekend.

Why?

First of all, when your skin is exposed to rays of light from the sun (even on a cloudy day), it forms vitamin D. Which is needed for your health and happiness.

Secondly, spending time in nature has proven to boost your mood *and* your immune system.

In Japan, they started a practice called forest bathing, whereby they spend a couple of days completely immersed in nature. Really soaking it up.

I've also come across studies suggesting that spending time in nature might help combat ADD/ADHD.

Recently, I read that spending as little as two hours a week in nature boosts your happiness.

Twenty minutes a day, in other words. More or less.

The cool thing? That's about the same amount you need to exercise. So if there's a park or garden where you live, you can kill two birds with one stone by going jogging. Or simply start biking or walking to school if you live in the countryside.

If you have a garden or a greenhouse, you can also sit there while reading or studying. If you're still focused on your phone even in the garden though, it might not do you as much good.

Live in the big city? Go for a long walk in the park or for a hike outside the city once a week. Or get yourself a balcony and fill it with as many plants as possible—though, most likely, you will still need to spend some time in real nature to reap all the benefits. Still, a green space can be very calming.

Then we have the dreaded winter blues. If you live in the north, you've probably experienced it. Perhaps you only feel a bit more tired or lethargic towards the end of winter; perhaps your mood tanks the moment fall makes its appearance. If that's the case, spending time outdoors might really help you. Getting special indoor lights that mimic the sun can also help.

If you suffer badly from the winter blues, speak with a professional. There are many other things you can do to boost your mood!

A NOTE ON SUNSHINE

Your skin needs sunlight, but it is also sensitive to it and too much exposure can cause cancer. So if you live in a hot place, spending time in the midday sun isn't the best idea. Choose to be outdoors early in the morning or late in the afternoon instead. If you are going to spend time in direct sunlight for longer periods of time, be sure to protect your skin. Interestingly, people in certain hot countries are vitamin D deficient because they avoid the sun so much!

If You Snooze, You Lose . . . or Not!

Sleep is essential . . . unless you want a poor immune system and a malfunctioning brain.

It's not just about getting the right amount of hours, but also *when* you go to sleep every day.

Ever had jet lag?

Stinks, doesn't it? You feel lethargic in the middle of the day. Can't sleep at night. Wake up at the wrong hour. Oversleep. Take your pick.

The thing is, if you go to bed at nine one day and eleven thirty the next, you will be jet lagged. It will just be much less obvious, but your body will still suffer.

Then, there's sleep quality. If you're watching a bright screen or have bright lights on until just when you fall asleep, your brain gets affected by the light. Your ability to go into deep sleep can take longer than normal. What's more, you might not even be able to fall asleep for some time. Tip: Read about the circadian rhythm and how it works.

All of this is why it's so important to have a sleep routine.

So what is a sleep routine?

It's a routine for going to bed that should happen around the same time every night.

At a certain hour, you turn the lights down (including the brightness of your screen if you're using an electronic device, one and a half to two hours before bed) and then, at least half an hour before bed, you turn the phone, tablet, TV, and computer off and turn the lights down further.

Just before bed, it's good to relax for half an hour, perhaps by reading a book, meditating, or doing something else that calms you. If you're reading a book on your phone or tablet, you can keep it on so long as it's in night mode and you're using a reading app where you control the color and brightness. Just remember to put the phone or tablet in flight mode as you don't want to get messages while you're relaxing.

It might seem strange not being online chatting with your friends just before bed, or checking social media, but if you do that, there's constantly new information. You're not truly relaxed. If you want to connect with someone, call them. That said, it's still good to have some time just for you before you snooze.

You might also wonder why you shouldn't be watching a movie for that last half an hour. Well, first of all, there's the screen brightness. Secondly, just as when chatting with lots of people or checking your social media, there's something happening. Your mind isn't relaxing; it's following a plot, and as the main character faces dangers or funny situations, you put yourself in their shoes. Meaning, your brain is wide awake. So try to keep the movie and social media to earlier in the evening.

But what about reading? Don't you get engrossed in the plot? Sure, but there's no moving imagery or sound, so it's more relaxing.

Having the same routine every night helps your body remember it's time for sleep. What's more, by turning the lights down, or off, some time before bed, your body starts producing more melatonin—the hormone that's needed for sleep.

But what about the weekend? Can't you stay up late some nights?

Sure you can. But try not to overdo it. For example, if you have a really late Friday, try to go to bed *closer* to your normal time on Saturday and get up around your normal time on a Sunday. Otherwise, chances are you'll feel sluggish come Monday.

How many hours of sleep do you need, anyway? If you're between 14–17, about eight to ten hours. If you're 18 or over, seven to nine hours.

CHEAT SHEET

- Dim your lights and turn down screen brightness if using electronic devices two to four hours before bed
- Turn off your phone, tablet, TV, and computer half an hour before bed—if you read on it, turn off your lights and turn on dark mode
- Get to bed around the same time every night
- Get up around the same time every night

You might ask yourself why this is so important. So what if you mess up your sleep a bit and are tired some days? Does it really matter?

Yes.

Poor sleep affects your immune system, cognitive functioning, and mood. Meaning, if you want to be happy and healthy (and find it easier to memorize things in school), good sleep is crucial. That doesn't mean you can't stay up late for parties or pull a late night when cramming for an exam. It just means that you should try to get a good night's sleep on most days.

LEARNING MORE

If you want to learn more about how sleep affects you, look up the circadian rhythm. You can also find out about natural ways to increase your melatonin levels if you find it difficult to fall asleep. Plus, there are some natural herbs people have used for centuries to improve sleep. However, you should never take herbs without consulting a doctor first.

The Power of Social Connections and Altruism

This is the part where I tell you to start flexing your kindness muscles.

Sort of.

The reason people live so long in the Blue Zones isn't just about the food. They tend to exercise a fair amount (but more as a social activity and necessity—such as walking to school or work—than going to the gym), don't lead stressful lives, and socialize a lot.

Did you know that people with a great social life tend to be happier and live longer?

Yup.

Which sort of stinks if you're currently at a school where you don't have that many friends. But that will change. You will go on to other schools or jobs. You will partake in hobbies where you'll meet like-minded people. And if socializing scares the living daylight out of you, read books about how to become a social ninja and sign up for workshops in social and people skills. You might also want to get a therapist who can help you understand why you're uncomfortable socializing and how to overcome it.

The thing is, some people are born into families where everyone is super social. They might also grow up in a natural circle of friends their parents introduced them to early on.

Others aren't that lucky. Circumstances (such as parents who aren't particularly great at people skills), early trauma, conditions such as autism, ADHD, or Asperger's might make socializing a lot harder—even painful at times.

Thankfully, some really smart people long ago realized that one can learn social skills. Today there are books, online courses, coaching, and so much more available. But if you want to start from scratch, you can read two of the first personal development books in this niche: *How to Make Friends and Influence People* by Dale Carnegie and *Psycho-Cybernetics* by Maxwell Maltz. These two books were written a long time ago but are still gold.

The books have somewhat different approaches—Carnegie offers more direct advice on how to have great people skills, while Maltz talks about how to improve your confidence in different areas which helps with people skills—but both are excellent books. And you'll be able to find plenty of sum-ups of them too, if you don't want to read them from cover to cover. There are even videos on YouTube—the books are tremendously popular. Personally, I listened to the audiobooks.

Want to meet more people? Here are some ideas:

1. Start taking classes in something you enjoy (dancing, tennis, drawing, etc.)
2. Do workshops in something you enjoy (like a weekend workshop in yoga)
3. Attend local events, such as festivals, fairs, and the like—you can also try to attend events outside your local area if you don't feel comfortable around the people in your hometown
4. Join a local book circle, hiking group, fishing community, the scouts, a baking society, or similar—you might even be able to find book clubs online if there's none near you
5. Volunteer at a charity (sometimes animal shelters and the like have special opportunities for youth)
6. When you're old enough, if you like it, you can start a business where you get to sell something at local markets or fairs—that will help you connect with other business owners and customers (make jam, paint rocks, sell everything in the garage, knit baby scarves, make wooden utensils, etc.)
7. Join online groups where you meet people with similar interests
8. If you are 18 or older, you can join Meetup.com and InterNations.org where you will find local meetups based around interests (from startup clubs, to meetups for people doing knitting, and everything in between)

I mentioned volunteering above, but this is so important I am going to talk about it more.

Why?

Well, some studies suggest that people who volunteer or get involved in some sort of charity work are happier and live longer. It is also an excellent opportunity to do something you love while forging bonds with other people in the organization.

For example, if you love horses, you can join a local charity that focuses on improving the lives of horses or that offers a sanctuary for horses.

Make sure you find a place where you truly get to do what you love (and aren't stuck calling around asking for donations if you hate sales).

Being part of a cause also adds meaning to our lives. We get to feel that we are making an impact. That we have the power to help others and the planet. And we do.

We are mighty powerful little creatures once we set our mind on something.

PART 2

LOVE AND RELATIONSHIPS

3

Developing Healthy Relationships

Tips on how to manage relationships with friends, bosses, teachers, and partners (and some conflict resolution tools, too)

If communication creates relationships, relationships control a lot of how your life *feels* and the *results* you get.

A good relationship with your parents will make you feel good when you're around them.

A good relationship with your boss will lead to a happy work life and (perhaps) to pay raises.

A good relationship with your local bus driver will lead to them smiling at you and you smiling at them every afternoon. And when you lose your bus card, you'll probably get a free ride.

Look, you're responsible for how you feel. If you walk into a room with ice queens and haughty kings, you can choose to think of them as silly and have a giggle. Or you can feel miserable as they're all looking at you like something the cat dragged in.

And just because you weren't born into royalty! How unfair. Life's unfair. You'll never win at this. You'll never find nice people to make friends with. You might as well give up.

How you choose to *look* upon things and *feel* about things is your choice. But creating great relationships makes it easier to feel good, as people, generally speaking, will act nicer towards you. And it helps you with other things as well, as seen in the examples above.

So how do you create great relationships?

Be of Service to Others

My coach has been banging this into my head for years: show up to be of service.

What does that mean?

You show up with a willingness to serve those around you. Go out of your way to assist them.

That does NOT mean you're there to solve their problems, take over their burdens, take responsibility for their lives, or run yourself ragged trying to "save" them. That's being a knight in shining armor and will most likely end with you feeling mistreated as you've taken away their responsibilities and put them on your shoulders. It's a heavy burden to bear and unless they start taking responsibility for their lives, their lives won't improve. You're just taking some of the edge off.

> You cannot save people from themselves, but you can assist them in saving themselves.

You can say, "I will go out of my way to explain to this drug addict about AA and the wonderful things that happened to a friend's parent who joined the program. I will even offer to drive them to the next meeting and call them once every couple of days to help inspire them to go to meetings." You cannot be responsible for them getting sober, on the other hand. That's their journey to walk. And if you decide to drive them to more than one meeting, you need to ensure it doesn't negatively impact your life. You can also set boundaries—offer to drive them for a month, then they're on their own.

That's a pretty extreme example. Let's just say that you're going to a party. You're thinking about how people will perceive you—if you're funny, if your outfit looks right, if you'll meet someone interesting and make a new friend, etc.

Instead, you could think, "I'm going to show up as my best self and give my best to others." That's being of service. Harping on about your latest soccer goals to impress others, on the other hand, is not being of service to them.

Being of service tends to take the ego out of things. "I'll show up at work doing my best and assisting in any way I can" as opposed to "I need to impress the new boss with my knowledge, speed, and personality." If you're doing your best, you'll still use your knowledge, speed, and personality to assist the company and your colleagues in any way possible, but you won't be petrified about them judging you. You're not doing it to prove yourself, but to serve the company.

This also helps when we get angry. For example, do I serve my kids by getting angry when they do something out of line? Or would explaining how I feel and why they shouldn't be doing what they're doing be better?

Taking responsibility for *my* emotions while, if relevant, explaining *why* the behavior they have doesn't serve them is likely going to help them a lot more, don't you think?

Let's look at an example. The kids are running late in the morning. Again. I am now missing ten minutes of my day. Again. By the end of the week, as a freelancer, I've missed fifty minutes. That's almost an hour's worth of pay. By the end of the month, that's four hours worth of pay. By the end of the year, over forty hours worth of pay.

That's why I *feel* irritated. I don't have to blame and shame them because I am irritated. Nor do I need to sugarcoat the fact that they need to take responsibility for their timekeeping if I am to give them a ride. If they don't, I won't drive them because it's negatively impacting *me*.

What's more, I can go out of my way to *serve* them by explaining *why* timekeeping is important.

I can explain to my kids that if they are not responsible with their time, they will miss out on things. If they are late to a job interview, chances are, they won't get the job. If they're constantly late to work, they might lose their job. And if they're a freelancer, they'll lose out on pay. Not to mention, dates might walk away if they're late for a date, as might friends if they don't show up on time for lunch. And if they're late for a flight, well . . . bye, bye.

If they are on time, it will serve me, and by extension, them. I work so we can have a home.

If they are on time, it will serve them. Because their future will likely look better once they learn to be on time.

If I continue to indulge them by waiting for them in the morning, it won't serve them. If I tell them that I will drive them on time in the future, they will learn to be on time, which will serve them.

However, I will have to tell them the above in a kindly manner if I want to receive a positive response (I don't mean trying to please them, I just mean not losing my cool). I can also tell them I have faith in them—I believe they can be on time. I am absolutely certain they have the power to do that.

Being of service is not about shaming and blaming others. Being of service is assisting them where we can by going out of our way to do so. If I'd just driven off in the car every morning without explanation to my kids, I wouldn't have taken the time to serve them.

Focus on the Positive in Others

This is a game-changer.

Your sister is annoying. So annoying. You keep telling her that. She gets more annoying.

Your sister is also good at giving compliments. She readily thanks you when you do something for her. She's an epic hugger. She always tidies up after herself. Without her, evenings would be boring.

Do you ever tell her that?

If you did, do you think she might act less annoying around you? Perhaps, she might even try to please you. When we are nice to people they are much more likely to be nice in return.

That doesn't mean your sister should get away with things. Tell her to stop doing whatever is annoying you (just like I told my kids to stop being late), but do it in a nice way. And *focus* on telling her as often as possible all the things she's great at and all that you *love* about her. If you can't manage the L word, try the other L word—*like*.

Nagging Doesn't Work

"Don't do that."

"You didn't take the rubbish out. Again. Will you ever do it?"

"You're always late. Stop being so late all the time."

You know the drill. Someone is driving you insane doing . . . or not doing . . . something.

And why are they still doing or not doing it? They should have learned by now.

Seriously. Why can't they just do what they're supposed to?

Here's a tip: Get them to do whatever it is you want them to do once, and praise them. Rain praise on their head. "It's so awesome you remembered to do the dishes today. That means I can relax after dinner. Thank you, thank you, thank you!" Show your joy. If possible, pat them on the back or hug them to reinforce the message.

It's called positive reinforcement. And it's the basis of many parenting techniques.

When you become a parent, you might want to scream, "NO, don't hit the child in the playground." You'll learn fast that it's much better to say, "Go play with them instead of hitting them. If you hit them, they'll be sad. If you play with them, they'll be happy and want to play more. You'll have more fun. Here, play with this ball. But remember, if you hit again, we go home immediately."

If they hit again? You go home. No arguments. No shaming and blaming. Just stating the facts: "You hit someone, it hurt them, now we have to leave as we can't be here if we hit people."

If they do as you asked and play nicely? By the end of the playtime, you jump up and down, screaming, "Yay, you played with them nicely and without hitting them. You made a new friend. You're so fantastic."

In the example above, you tell the child that if they hit again, they will be punished by being taken home instead of getting to play more. That sets a clear *boundary*.

But you also clarify *what you want them to do*, and when they do it, you *reward them* by hugging them and telling them they are so good for having done the right thing. And here, you have to spell out what the right thing is, "You didn't hit them, you played nicely, you're awesome." Just saying "Well done" doesn't do it as it doesn't relate back to what you asked of them.

Another example would be if your friend constantly borrows something from you and forgets to hand it back. "You forgot to bring me my game. Again. It's really irritating. I lent you the game and you're being an idiot not bringing it back when I ask you," might be what you want to tell them.

Instead, you can say, "Can you please bring me my game tomorrow? If I am to lend you things again, you have to respect me when I want them back, or I can't keep lending you things. And hey, if you do bring it tomorrow, I'll lend you that other game you wanted." Once they hand it back, you thank them profusely, and either slap them on the back or hug them, and give them the other game.

If they don't give you back the game right away, you don't lend them any more games. At least not for a set period of time.

If they don't seem to want to hand back the game at all? You have to tell your or their parents to do something about it.

Good relationships are all about boundaries, being clear on what you expect, and telling people when you're happy about something they've done or said.

In short, the more you *clarify the behavior you want* (instead of harping on about the negative behavior) and *reward that behavior*, the more incentivized people are to do as you say.

If you give someone attention, even negative attention, when they do something, chances are they'll keep doing it.

The main thing to remember is to focus on teaching people what you *want* them to do, not what you *don't* want them to do. And then you have to *reward* them when they do what you want them to. And by reward, I mean to thank them, praise them, and preferably, do something like hug them, shake their hand, or pat them on the back to truly reinforce the message.

When people feel nagged at, or like you're constantly dissing them, they don't respond favorably when you ask them to do things.

Let's reverse the situation.

Your dad keeps telling you to study for tests. All the time. What can you do to deal with it?

"Dad, I really appreciate you wanting me to do well in school. I find it a bit hard to hear you ask me about it all the time, though. Could you perhaps, instead, encourage me to study by asking me about my studies? Tell me you think I'll do well at the next test when you see me studying? And celebrate with me when I do well on a test? I'd like to share the study journey with you, just in a different way."

Of course, the moment your dad asks about your studies *without* nagging you, you have to thank him for it. When he celebrates your victories on tests, you have to thank him for it.

You could also tackle this with the positive feedback sandwich.

The Positive Feedback Sandwich

The moment you accuse anyone of anything, they become defensive, walk away, or sort of block you out.

Shaming, blaming, guilting . . . if you do that to someone, they put their fences up, so to speak.

Imagine your parent telling you, "You need to learn to handle your sister better. You always snap at her. It's time you learned to control your emotions and act like the fifteen-year-old you are. She's only five."

What do you want to do?

Defend yourself, of course! You might even shift the blame to your sister.

"Don't just blame me. Talk to her about it. She's the one making me snap."

Imagine instead your parent saying, "I really love how you handle your little brother. Can you also handle your sister like that? You praise your brother when he does something nice and are also firm when he does something naughty, but you don't get upset. With your sister, you get very frustrated and sometimes snap at her. Can you try to handle her more the way you do your brother? And by the way, I was also impressed with your test score the other day."

This kind of "pro, con, pro" approach disarms people. While if you come at them with an "accusation" (something that needs to change), their guard immediately goes up.

You can use this in the example above with your dad nagging you. "Dad, I appreciate you really care about my studies. I'd also appreciate it if you don't always ask me if I have studied—I normally do, and I'd love it if you could acknowledge that. By the way, I really enjoyed that soccer game we had last week."

Whenever you get annoyed with something someone is doing, think "pro, con, pro" and come up with something positive before you tackle what you want to see change. That way, you can explain the behavior you want them to have . . . and then reward it when it happens!

You can use the same approach when giving feedback if you're coaching a team of soccer players, mentoring a student, or supervising someone at work.

For example, "I really like how you handled that customer complaining about the ice cream machine breaking down. You were a bit slow with the flipping of the burgers, think we can improve that tomorrow? I'd appreciate it. The faster you flip, the more money we make. Oh, and good job with the tills. I know they can be tricky to learn how to use, but you're acing it." This person is likely to show up very motivated to flip burgers fast as anything the following day. And when they do . . . you rain praise on them. You might even reward them with a bonus or a free meal. That way, their motivation to keep flipping burgers fast will increase.

Please note that this isn't about manipulating people to do whatever you want them to do. This is about dealing with stuff that needs to be dealt with.

It's not helpful if your little sister is annoying you to get a rise out of you. (Negative attention.)

It's not helpful if your dad nags you about homework all the time.

It's not helpful if you snap at your little sister.

It's not helpful if your friend borrows games from you and "forgets" to hand them back.

You need to establish clear boundaries. Sometimes it helps if you explain your boundary using a positive feedback sandwich.

When a person performs the behavior that's helpful—for them or for you—you reward it. That way, they're more motivated to keep on doing it.

Responding to Criticism and Conflict

Let's say it's you that's, so to speak, under attack. In other words, someone is frustrated, angry, or upset with you. Perhaps they are even feeling hurt by something you've done, be it that you did it intentionally or not.

Let's say your mother flips one night when you rise from the table after dinner, take your phone out of your pocket to check for messages, and forget to say thanks for the meal as you amble off to put the dishes in the sink while looking at the phone.

Your mother says, "That's it, I've had it. You're constantly on that phone, not caring about anyone else. You can't even say thank you for the meal. You're off to chat to someone on social media instead. Give me the phone, it's gone for the night."

Here, chances are your mother feels underappreciated. She's cooked a meal for you. Before that, she was working to earn money to buy that meal. She got up early that morning to ensure you got up in time for school, and she made you breakfast. She ensures you get to school. Her life revolves around looking after you, even if she loves her job, her friends, and her partner. She's tired after a long day, and this is the proverbial drop that makes the beaker overflow.

You, in return, shout something to her about how unfair she is. Maybe you've not thanked her as much as usual because you're kind of upset with her about something else. Then, perhaps, you add how stressed and irritable she's been as of late. And what about that one time when she did that horrible thing and . . .

Suddenly, this isn't about you not saying "thank you" after dinner but all your past hurts and upsets.

That's mistake number one.

Mistake number two is to get defensive.

You want to make your mother happy and get the phone back?

"Sorry, Mom, I appreciate you worked hard to cook dinner. And I enjoyed the meal. I should have shown more gratitude. I love you and what you do for me. I confess to using my phone too much. Perhaps we can agree that I don't open the phone until *after* I get into my room from now on? If you want to keep the phone now, fine, but can I please answer some messages before bed? I'd appreciate it. I'll even do your dishes as well as mine. And I really do appreciate you, Mom."

Probably that'd be broken up into two—the second part where you negotiate about the phone might be after your mother's response to the part where you apologize, show you do have gratitude, and suggest that from now on, you won't open the phone until you're in your bedroom.

In short, own what you did wrong, apologize, and then tackle what you'd want to change in the other person's approach. It could be about the phone. It could also be about how your mother reacted. Perhaps she often "flips a switch" and gets angry.

To approach that, you could try, "Sorry, Mom, I appreciate you worked hard to cook dinner. And I enjoyed the meal. I should have shown more gratitude. I love you and what you do for me. I confess to using my phone too much. Perhaps we can agree that I don't open the phone until *after* I get into my room from now on?" Then your mother responds to that. "Can I also say I felt hurt when you yelled at me like that? Can we both try to speak calmly when we are upset? I know we won't always succeed, but can we try? It would make me feel better."

You've taken responsibility for your part and apologized. Now you're asking your mom to take responsibility for her part. Doing it that way is much more likely to resolve the conflict than screaming at your mother for screaming at you. That will only make things worse.

Another approach to resolving conflict is to acknowledge what the other person is upset about even if you *don't* agree.

"You're constantly late, and when you come home, you spend all your time in your room. You don't appreciate our family. I'm disappointed in you."

Whoa, the venom coming your way. Your parent is really upset. And for what? You've been studying at school and staying late so you can get to college. Earn some money. Enough to look after your parents when they get old. You've been in your room studying or spending a little time chatting to friends to finally relax after a long day. Your parent just isn't being fair with you.

So you get angry. And shout back.

Or, even as you feel your anger and the unfairness of it all, you take a deep breath. "If I understand you correctly, you're upset because I come home late and spend a lot of time in my bedroom. You feel that because I do that, I'm ignoring our family and that I'm being disrespectful and impolite. In other words, I don't show that I care about you enough. Is that correct?"

If your parent confirms this, you say, "I hear what you're saying. The reason I've come home late and spent time in my bedroom is to study. At night, I also take half an hour to chat with friends as I spend all afternoon and most of the night studying. It's my way to relax. I study so I can get to college and make a living. I hope to help you guys financially when I'm older, too. So I do not mean to be disrespectful. If anything, I'm trying my best to respect this family and everything you've taught me by making something out of myself."

Can you see how you've not only disarmed the unhappy parent, but also shown how much you do care for them? While simultaneously defending what you're doing without being defensive?

Now, if we are to take this one step further, you can offer to spend more time with your family one day a week. Such as on a Sunday morning when you usually go for a jog but could go for a walk with them instead. Or whatever it might be.

Some of these answers are stuffy. You have to speak using your vocabulary . . . when one writes, one tends to put things a bit differently.

Let's break this down.

When you get "attacked," try to hear what the other person is saying:

- They are upset, why?
- Have they woven a meaning into something you did that isn't true?
- Are they right in what they say but saying it in the wrong way?

Take a moment. Breathe. Then sum up what they are saying. "If I understand you right . . ." "Am I right in thinking you mean . . ."

Then acknowledge whatever wrongs you did, "I understand why you feel that way, and I'm sorry for what I did. In the future, I will consider how it makes you feel and . . ." You can also add an, "I can't go back in time and change it, but maybe I can do X to at least try to make it up to you?"

Or, if they've done a mindread (which we'll talk more about in chapter 5), "I understand it might be interpreted that way, and why you're upset, but that's not why I did it . . ."

Then, move on to how you want to deal with conflict in the future. "In the future, when either one of us gets upset, can we try to talk to each other calmly? Without blaming or shaming one another? Or dragging up old hurts? I know it's hard. I know I won't be able to always stay calm. But maybe we can help each other? Encourage each other?" (You don't have to say all of that—only the part which bugs you, perhaps it's just the shouting, perhaps it's that they start talking about all your character flaws . . . whatever it might be!)

Apart from throwing in old hurts when one gets upset, it's easy to walk off and shut the other person out. Unfortunately, that doesn't resolve the conflict. If anything, it lets things fester and grow. So, if you feel you need to step aside, say that. "I'm sorry, but I'm feeling really upset at what you said. I know you might not have meant to upset me, but please give me a moment before we speak. I'm just gonna go for a walk or listen to some music or something to calm my thoughts. Then I can talk to you about this, and we can resolve it."

It will go against every instinct you have to stay calm when someone is accusing you of something, shaming you, blaming you, or simply being upset with you.

Defend.

Attack back.

Or retreat.

That's what you'll want to do.

If you do that, the conflict is likely to remain unsolved or escalate.

Resolving conflict takes strength.

You have to take responsibility for your part and apologize.

If you actually didn't do anything wrong, you have to ask if you understood the other person correctly and explain back to them why you think they're upset.

You have to explain why what you did wasn't meant to hurt them.

You have to ask for what you want in the future.

Likewise, it takes strength not to scream and shout, blame, shame, attack, or do something of the sort when you are upset with someone for doing something. Instead, you have to calmly explain how you feel and ask if things could be done differently in the future. You might even have to think about their positive traits and use a positive feedback sandwich to get through to them. That's not easy when you're really upset.

In the chapter about emotional management, I'll teach you how to help yourself in controlling your response to just about anything.

Stating Things in the Positive

The positive feedback sandwich is when you have to point out something negative, but do it by saying something positive before or after handing out criticism so that the person doesn't get offended. But sometimes you don't need to talk about the negative, only shift it to the positive.

No, that's not a math equation.

Let's say your gran always buys you a gift that has something to do with soccer for Christmas because when you were younger, you played soccer. Only you don't play anymore and don't want any more gifts related to soccer.

If you tell your gran that you don't like her gifts, how will she feel? Not great, right?

But if you instead tell her you've started playing basketball and talk about how much you want her to buy some basketball-related gift for Christmas, chances are she'll want to please you and will get you the gift you asked for. But if you tell her that last year's gift was horrific . . . well, she will feel sad and possibly angry.

Now, I'm not saying you shouldn't be honest about something that's bugging you. If your gran just got you a gift you don't like, you can just as easily say, "I really appreciate the thought you put into our gifts, Gran. I've started playing more basketball recently, so would you mind if we exchange it for something related to that instead? Maybe you could come with me and we could make a day out of it?"

Note that not even in that example do you say you don't like your gran's gift. Instead, you say you appreciate her and explain what you want (instead of harping on about what you don't want). If you add some enthusiasm into the mix and show your gran you truly care about her, it will go down even better.

We often hurt people's feelings if we blurt out what we don't like about them or what they do or what we get from them. That's why it's good to ask for what you want instead of criticizing what you don't want.

Simply remember to state things in the positive.

This isn't only when you want to point out something you want someone to do differently; it also applies when chatting to new people, writing emails, writing profiles, and so forth. Think about how you phrase things.

"I just hate waiting in line, I don't go to restaurants where the waiters are lazy."

"I just love fast service. I go to restaurants where the service is good so I can walk away happy."

"I don't want to become friends with liars. They get me down."

"I really want to make friends with honest people. It makes life so much easier and more fun."

Depending on what you choose to say, people will view you differently. I always tell people this is really important when writing dating profiles online. If you talk about everything you don't want, or don't like, people write you off as grumpy or difficult.

In general, when you talk about things, if you add a touch of positivity, people will be more drawn to you. And, chances are, you'll see yourself in a better light.

"I had some challenges in my teens and uh, yeah, I got through them. Now I'm, uh, okay."

"I had some challenges in my teens that taught me so much about life. Now I use what I learned, and I think it's made me a better person."

"I made a mistake, I'm horrible."

"I made a mistake, which shows I'm trying things out and learning. It means I'm growing and moving forward. If I just sat on my backside doing nothing, I'd never mess up and never grow."

This is about communication, but it's also about relationships—with yourself and others. When being positive in your communication, you uplift others, as well as yourself.

Embracing Flaws in Yourself and Others

No one is perfect.

Even the people who love you the most will make mistakes—and by doing so, let you down. But if they love you, they'll be willing to do their best not to make the same mistakes again and probably try to make it up to you.

Still, no one is exactly like you, which means there will always be conflict. My principal at drama school used to say that even in the greatest of love stories, Romeo wants five kids and Juliet only one. To Romeo, Juliet only wanting one child is a flaw. To Juliet, Romeo wanting five kids is a flaw. Though technically, of course, these preferences aren't flaws. Just a difference in opinion. But let's face it: we all have real flaws. We are grumpy at night . . . or in the morning. We can never remember where we put the keys. We spend more money than we should on shoes or traveling. Some of these flaws we work to fix, others we don't care so much about.

My point is:

> There will always be conflict in relationships because people want different things and no one is perfect.
>
> And remember that just because you want something out of a relationship, it doesn't mean the other person wants the same thing. They might not even be capable of giving it.

Your best friend wants to spend every Sunday with you, but you only want to spend every other Sunday with them as there are other things you want to do some Sundays. On the flip side, you might want them to come to your soccer matches, but they might have other plans on those days. You have to find out what works for both of you and see if that is enough to remain friends.

Plus, everyone has an annoying habit, or two. Some people talk incessantly when they get nervous. Some people crack the wrong joke at the wrong time over and over again. Some people seem unable to be on time.

When you become friends with people, work with them, or enter into a romantic relationship with them, you have to decide up front if you're going to accept their flaws or if some things are deal breakers. Because always nagging or being miserable because they aren't the person you want them to be isn't going to help.

For example, you accept that your boss is a bit grumpy (especially on Monday mornings) because they are generally easy to work with and pay you well. But if your boss suddenly becomes really rude and is constantly reprimanding you, you realize it's unhealthy to be around them. So you tell them that either they change their ways or you leave.

Even the nicest people say and do the wrong thing when under pressure or are simply uninformed. That's why I said earlier that everyone will let you down at some point, because they're human—they make mistakes. The good ones work hard not to repeat them.

Some people aren't able to control themselves—there are several mental health conditions that might make you more impulsive, prone to anger, and so forth. However, if someone isn't willing to get help, then you have to ask yourself if it's worth sticking around or if doing so is compromising your happiness.

In a sense, your relationship with yourself is the same. There are flaws you have that you are okay with (you can't be bothered to change your habits of throwing dirty clothes on the floor instead of in the laundry bin). There are others you aren't okay with (it's not alright to be so lazy you never exercise).

Have compassion for yourself—we aren't born with all the answers (meaning we will make mistakes) and we all have flaws we need to work through. Have the same compassion for others but also know when to put your foot down. And remember—you don't have to berate someone for what they are doing wrong, simply tell them what you'd like them to do instead. That's more likely to lead to a good chat than telling them they're horrible for doing x, y, z.

Strategies for De-escalation and Calmness

You get a text from your friend saying they aren't coming to your birthday party. They've been flaky lately. They also seem uninterested in speaking with you at school. You blow your fuse and text back that if they don't want to see you anymore, what's the point in being friends?

The two of you stop speaking.

Then you realize their dad was diagnosed with a disease. They've been distant because they were not dealing with it very well. They didn't want to speak about it but didn't know what else to say because that's all they thought about. They randomly canceled things to be with their dad.

Now, first of all, there was mind reading happening. You didn't ask your friend *why* they couldn't come to your birthday or why they've been flaky and aloof at school. You made it mean something. That's why you were angry. And then you reacted to that anger. You didn't react to them saying they couldn't make it to your birthday party; you reacted to what you made that *mean*. You thought it meant they don't want to be your friend anymore. That they don't like you anymore. That they aren't worth it because they're not showing up anymore.

If you have an intense emotional reaction to something, don't respond to it right away. Whether it's your mother saying something that makes you angry or you feel let down by a friend, don't speak or write when you're upset. Go for a walk. Watch a show. Talk to someone else. At the very least, take ten deep breaths (though usually that's not enough to shift out of an emotion).

First, ask yourself why you're feeling that way. When we are prickly (and we all have days like that) and when we've been hurt a lot in the past, we tend to overreact. If two other friends before the one mentioned above started becoming flaky and then stopped speaking with you, it's natural that when a third person goes aloof, you put meaning into it. But even though it's natural that you think they don't want to be your friend anymore because of what's happened in the past, it's not necessarily the truth.

So, always ask yourself if you're making something mean more than it does, or if you know for sure that you've interpreted the situation correctly.

Lastly, ask yourself what you want the outcome to be.

If, in the example above, you wanted your friend to affirm that they care about you and want to stay friends with you, then what should your text message really have read? Perhaps, "Alright, I'm sorry you can't come. I was really looking forward to having you there. In fact, I feel a bit upset you can't make it as you've seemed distant lately and canceled a lot of things. Have I done something to upset you? Or is something else wrong? Or do you just not want to be friends anymore? Please let me know. Hugs."

Look, maybe that's a bit formal, but imagine if you broke stuff down like that—asking yourself why you're reacting the way you do and if you've weaved meaning into the situation, and then asking yourself what you want the outcome to be and acting on that instead of the hurt. Imagine if *everyone* broke stuff down like that. How many fights and misunderstandings could be avoided?

Of course, some people act out without knowing why. You can ask your friend the above, but they might just reply, "I'm just not feeling it lately." That does not reassure you that they care about you. It won't tell you what's wrong, if anything. It won't give you anything to work with. And you'll have to accept that sometimes. You can prod if it's someone close to you, but not all people are aware of why they feel and act the way they do.

Your friend might feel your friendship is starting to fizzle out. Perhaps you're both changing. But they don't even think that far. They just aren't feeling it. Or they might not be open to communication.

Remember what I said above about deal breakers, though? If someone becomes super flaky then perhaps it's time to move on.

All relationships aren't meant to last. More on that in the next chapter.

Loving People "Their Way" Is a Thing

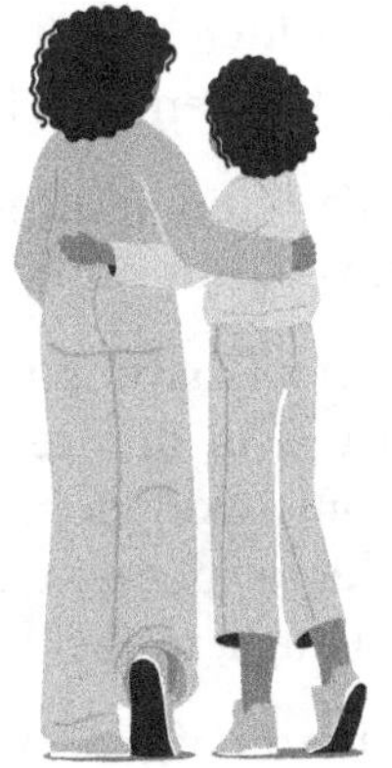

You meet a great person. You have so much in common. You instantly like one another, perhaps even feel like you love one another. Surely your relationship will just magically work out, whether it's a friendship or something romantic.

No.

They are a great person. That doesn't make them great at *relationships*.

You have a lot in common, but they want to pursue a whirlwind career in New York and you want a farm in Italy.

It's not just about meeting someone great whom you have things in common with. It's about creating a) a great relationship and b) a life that you can continue to share. With friends, the latter is easier—you can email each other from across the world and go for visits. But for a romantic relationship, you usually need to want a similar lifestyle . . . in the same place.

The thing with building great relationships is that it takes a lot of communication. Your friend or partner won't know how you wish to be treated. You have to tell them.

Likewise you have to ask someone how they want to be treated.

Imagine you've moved to a new town a few months back and become really close with this one friend. Their birthday is coming up, and you know they've said they really long to go on a road trip. So you decide to make it happen.

You're not much for planning; you prefer adventure. So what you do is pack a suitcase, rent a car, and have a loose plan of where you're going. You've got your GPS and a credit card, what else could you need? You'll have fun finding places to stay along the way.

When you pick your friend up on their birthday and shout "Surprise! We're not going for cake, we're going on a road trip," they don't react as you imagined. Instead of being happy that you're paying for a road trip, they start fretting about not having had time to pack, and when you say you don't have an itinerary set in stone, they grow pale.

They're the kind of person who needs to plan everything in advance. They want to know down to the last detail what's going to happen. To you, that seems silly. You want adventure.

On another note, your friend feels loved when you tell them how and why you love them, while you think spending quality time with you should make them feel loved.

We often assume people will feel loved when we do what makes us feel loved. But other people are not like us.

Gary Chapman points out in *The Five Love Languages* that people *feel* loved in different ways. Some like to receive gifts, others compliments. Some like people to show love by doing things for them, while others just like to spend quality time together. Yet others need physical contact, such as hugs, to feel loved.

On top of that, we all have different needs in life.

In the example above, I made you a spontaneous adventurer and your friend a planner seeking security. When we spend a lot of time with someone, we have to learn about their needs and share our own.

So communicate what you want and need. Ask people close to you what they want and need. Acknowledge they might need things you can't provide. Is that a deal-breaker or not?

If you get upset, communicate it without blame. Remember what I wrote earlier about stepping away, breaking it down, and approaching them from a positive angle? Don't make up what their actions mean—ask them what they mean.

When they speak, listen. Really listen.

And as for the loving each other part, figure out what they need to feel loved. Is it words of affirmation? Is it physical touch (like hugs)? Is it gifts? Is it acts of service (like bringing them a takeaway coffee when they are studying)? Is it quality time (like doing things together)?

TIPS

Go to www.5lovelanguages.com and take the quiz! The results may surprise you or confirm what you already know. And remember, your actual relationship with other people is the best way to figure out *how* people need to be loved.

Remember YOU

Here's the deal—the most attractive people lead lives they enjoy. That's why they're attractive. It's almost as if they become magnetic—people want to get to know them.

That doesn't just go for romantic relationships, but for friendships. Someone who has a schedule packed with things that make them happy is, generally speaking, very happy. Which makes them come across as fun and interesting.

So do that—pack your schedule with things you love; things that make you happy.

Friends and dates won't make you feel as good as a good relationship with yourself will.

Figure out the things you love doing and start doing them. And when you meet fantastic people, stick to your guns about those things. Don't stop going to the gym, taking salsa classes, seeing other friends, and so forth just because you met someone else who is interesting. Don't change your diary around for them until you know they're worth it. And even then, make sure you have time to pursue the things in life that matter to you and keep your other friendships alive.

Another thing that helps keep you on track with putting yourself first and leading a happy life is goals. Daily, achievable goals. More on that in the last chapters of this book, but suffice it to say—creating long-term goals that are broken down into daily tasks (that you celebrate when you achieve) are a brilliant way of keeping yourself on track. If you notice suddenly that you're spending all your time with your friends and none of your goals are being achieved . . . well, then it's time to change things around.

To create healthy relationships, you need to stay true to who you are and spend time doing things you love and that take you to the places you want to go in life. If you don't, you'll feel as if you're losing your identity and your life starts circling around just your friends or partner. And in the long run, that won't make you happy.

Also, remember that people do need to prove themselves. Someone can tell you that you are amazing, but how much time and effort have they put into your relationship to prove it? Don't get swept away, take things slow when getting to know new people.

Get the Help You Need, When You Need It

Do you get angry needlessly at people?

Does it seem you're always starting fights?

Are you super shy around people?

Do you always feel ashamed of yourself?

Do you struggle to make friends?

Do you have inappropriate thoughts about people?

Does your mood seem to go up and down like a yoyo?

Don't be ashamed. Something might have happened to cause this. Just get help. So it stops.

And know that you can get help anonymously from a counselor, therapist, psychologist, and so forth. Find someone with a good reputation, and get the help you need to overcome whatever is holding you back.

Getting the tools you need to become your best self is the most empowering thing you can do. It makes you a stronger person. Everyone has good and bad sides to their personality. The strong people take action to further improve the good and lessen the bad.

Is it unfair that some people don't seem to go through as much trauma and therefore don't have scars as big as yours to work through?

Sure it is.

Is it unfair that some people are born with a certain brain chemistry or genetic makeup that makes them more prone to being calm, happy, and socially adjusted?

Sure it is.

But it's the brave people who face their flaws and make the most out of life who can shine a light for the thousands, or millions, of other people who are in the same boat. Be that person. You have no idea how many other people you can inspire simply by taking that one step and getting the help you need to feel awesome.

4

Ending Relationships on a Good Note

Learning when to walk away and how to cope

Some relationships should end—they are not good for you, or they aren't good for your friend (mentor, partner, whoever it might be), or both.

Other relationships end because you grow apart and one or both of you feel that it's no longer working.

Yet, other relationships end because you move away from one another or a person passes away.

While the previous chapters talk a lot about how to create and maintain healthy relationships, this chapter deals mainly with when to end a relationship and how to cope with ending a relationship.

Not All Relationships Are Made to Last

I remember picking up a book by the Dalai Lama in my teens or twenties and browsing it at the library. It said something about humans changing and growing throughout life and therefore changing relationships.

In short, the Dalai Lama was saying that many relationships don't last because we grow apart from people.

It went against my romantic nature.

I wanted to get married and stay with the same man throughout life.

Looking back, I'm not the same person I was when I was browsing through that book. Sure, I have the same core—I still love poetry, filmmaking, baking, and traveling. I still write, take photos, and draw. But I have changed. I have developed as a human. My relationship skills, for one, are a lot better. So, it stands to reason that the people I attract are better. Some of my old friends evolved too. We're still friends. Some fell away by the roadside.

Relationships work when you evolve together. They don't usually work if you evolve at different rates or in different directions.

And that's fine. Because you want to be with people whom you gel with, and you will find them.

Again and again.

That's not to say that we don't all mourn when we lose friends. Sure we do. That's normal. But we have to remember that we will meet more fabulous humans. And what we think is great today will look like a horror scenario tomorrow. Because by then, we've discovered something even greater. No matter how unlikely that might seem *right now*.

When to Walk Away

You won't be a match for everyone. The more true you are to yourself, the more likely you are to meet the right people and bond with them. That said, sometimes, as I mentioned, people develop in different directions. At other times, people derail.

The nice friend you have right now might turn bitter and act out against people ten years from now if they don't learn how to manage their life.

Other times, someone's nice at first, but the more you get to know them, the more you discover you aren't compatible. Or they simply have one or two sides to their personality that are a deal-breaker to you. Perhaps they like to create conflict and being around them gets difficult as they seem to set off fires wherever they go. Or they're forever complaining about something.

On the flip side, it might be them who'll realize you aren't their cup of tea. You like them, but they aren't that into you. Then you have to remember that there are a ton of other people in this world who will like you. And your time is better spent with them than with someone who is lukewarm towards you.

There are also people who simply aren't worth it. Perhaps they're fun to hang out with, but they just aren't interested in building a great friendship or relationship. They like you, but as they aren't invested in creating a great relationship, you're better off having them as an acquaintance than as a close friend or partner.

> People have to be willing to go the extra mile to build great relationships.

When You Should Leave in a Hurry

Someone physically assaults you (and not because you hit them first).

Someone tells you you're a horrible person over and over again, in different ways.

Someone takes digs at your style, personality, friends, family, whatever it might be, on a regular basis.

Someone is always there, then withdraws, then pops back up again (and not just once—it's a pattern).

Someone gets physically close to you inappropriately (i.e. it's not your boy/girlfriend trying to kiss you OR it's your boy/girlfriend trying to kiss you when you've said NO). You do not need to sit close to anyone, hug anyone, or do anything else that you dislike just because they're your friend.

Someone is continuously canceling on you (and not because they're working at the ER and are on call).

Someone tries to press you to do things you do not wish to do (and I don't mean encouraging you to do better at school or join a soccer team with them).

Sometimes these things don't happen consistently. For example, someone tells you that you are wonderful. Amazing. They buy you gifts. They go out with you. It lasts a month. Then they spend a week telling you how you've let them down. How you are not good-looking enough. That you don't wear the right clothes. That you should do or be something else. Then they go back to being nice. A month later, they're back to putting you down.

Anyone can make a mistake and say something rude, or get a bit overly enthusiastic about something you don't want to do, but if it happens repeatedly—even if there are long periods of it not happening—it's a pattern.

Unfortunately, abusers tend to have this behavior. They're good to you, then they're bad to you, then they're good to you. You fear walking away because you will miss the good times. But you can be around people who are *consistently* good to you, and you deserve that. So don't be afraid to drop the abusers and move on. And if they start to threaten you when you try to leave, immediately get help. I can't emphasize this enough—you need to seek help immediately if someone threatens you, be it a friend, relative, partner, or even a co-worker.

Of course, people have bad days, bad weeks, and bad months. They can be prickly. And everyone says something they regret at some point or other. But if someone *keeps* putting you down one way or another, you have to explain to the person what they are doing and give them a chance to change, and leave if they don't. Or leave right away. You don't owe it to people to accept their bad behavior.

If someone is in any way threatening, you have to speak with an adult about it immediately. You should not deal with it alone for safety reasons. What's more, you will do well to have someone else guide you and lift you up.

If you feel bullied by someone and they don't back off when you tell them to stop, get help. Your goal in life is to surround yourself with as many fabulous people as possible. They will lift you up and carry you to heights you yourself might not even have realized existed. So if someone is pulling you down instead of lifting you up, it's time to leave. Even if they, at one point, made you feel fantastic. If you want, you can give them an option to change, but if they don't want to, then it's time to say goodbye.

NOTE

If anyone consistently abuses you, whether physically or mentally, seek assistance. Reach out to a parent, teacher, adult whom you trust, counselor, or even the police. Even if this person is sometimes nice or loves you, you still need to seek help. Now.

Why Love at First Sight Isn't Always True Love

You see someone at an event and immediately, you feel an urge to connect with them. So you do. And it turns out you have lots in common. Once you get to know them better, you also realize that there are lots of things you don't have in common. And that's the deal—we're attracted to people for a reason, but that reason isn't always enough to create a great friendship, or relationship.

The person you met might share your interests but aren't a great friend. Then it won't work out. Friendship won't be possible, at least not one where you're happy. Perhaps you can still enjoy them as an acquaintance, but you can't shape people into what you want them to be.

Other times, you realize that the person who, when out and about in public, is super charismatic and wonderful isn't all that wonderful when you're alone with them. They're plain boring.

There are a million reasons why we feel drawn to someone—it could be their looks, their charisma, their interests, or even their flaws—but that pull we feel isn't always a sign that they are our soulmate or twin flame.

Be careful when you feel pulled to connect with someone—connect and enjoy it, but don't fool yourself into believing you've met your next best friend or partner. Take your time to get to know them. Enjoy getting to know them. Just don't get carried away by hope.

Moving Forward When a Relationship Ends

The end of a relationship, be it a friendship or a romantic relationship, isn't the be-all and end-all of your life, but it can feel that way.

You've lost a special person. Whether you've lost them due to them moving, dying, breaking it off, or something else doesn't matter as much as the fact that the relationship you had is gone. You can no longer relate to them the way you used to, or you can't relate to them at all as they are no longer there.

You can't have that person back. Their unique personality, love, and approach to life ... you miss it. In fact, you might miss it so much you want to sit down and never get up again.

That's the way it feels.

That feeling will change.

As discussed in another chapter, you have to face the feeling. Then you have to move on to do other things. You cannot wallow in it.

Your life is not about one person and one person only. Slowly and surely, happiness will return to your life. If you let it.

Some of the best advice you'll ever get, as mentioned in a previous chapter, is to always lead a varied life. Take a class in something you enjoy so you meet people outside your regular circle of friends on a regular basis. Make it a point to see different friends and family members on a weekly basis. Have a routine where you set aside time for exercise and self-care. Have life and career goals that you take small daily steps toward. Never ever give your entire diary up for one person. Even if they are the greatest person alive, you still need to have other people in your life.

What's more, when you feel down in the dumps because a relationship ended, remember the mood boosters mentioned in chapter 1. Make sure you apply them.

You won't want to.

When you feel like crap, you don't want to do anything. Or you want to do all the wrong things.

Don't.

Instead, get up and do the stuff you love. Eventually, you will feel happiness again. Keep at it. Don't give up. Don't give in. Keep going. And if you need support, get it. Call a friend, a hotline, a therapist (great if you can afford it as they offer professional advice and can guide you in a way a friend can't), or someone else who can help uplift you if you need it.

And while you might not be able to imagine it yet, life is filled with people to love who will love you. There are millions of wonderful people just waiting for you to open your heart wide enough to discover them. People who might even be better than the one you lost even if you can't possibly imagine that right now.

PART 3

COMMUNICATING AND CONNECTING

5

Mastering Real World Conversation

What you say and don't say when using your body and words

Have you ever considered that if you can't communicate with people, you can't do very much at all? Making friends, holding down jobs, creating great relationships—it all comes down to communication.

So does negotiating better pay, maintaining relationships with co-workers, and making your parents more amenable to you staying up late on a Saturday night or attending that workshop you really want to go to.

In fact, almost everything in life is about communication. So let's have a look at how you can ace it!

Face-to-Face Communication

As humans, we communicate through language, right? The written and spoken word, as well as sign language.

Wrong.

Okay, not completely. We *do* communicate through words or signs. But we also communicate through other means. In fact, it's believed that up to 90% of communication is non-verbal.

Yep. 90%!

So what is non-verbal communication?

It's your facial expressions, body language, and your tone of voice. Sometimes all three are simply described as body language. And some people like to include your heart rate and breathing rate as those, too, communicate how you feel.

For example, your baby sister is asked by one of your parents (I refer to them as parents in this book, but it could be your guardian, grandparent, or anyone else who is caring for you) where their candy has disappeared to. Your sister squirms, looks at the floor, and says in a low voice that she has no idea.

Do you believe her? Or do you think, perhaps, she took the candy and is now feeling sheepish about it?

Let's say instead that she squares her shoulders, crosses her arms, and looks your parent straight in the eye, says in a loud voice, "I have no idea as I never saw the candy in the first place."

Do you believe her? Or is she covering up that she took the candy by being defensive?

Chances are, you aren't even consciously thinking about people's body language; you just make snap decisions about how you *feel* about them based on how they look and how they behave.

Decoding Body Language

Some people are so good at reading body language and facial expressions they're hired by the police to figure out if people are telling the truth during interrogations simply by looking at them when they speak.

You might not want to join the law enforcement, but it could be useful to figure out if your next date is interested in you or not!

Likewise, it's useful to learn what *you* communicate to others.

Chances are, you don't think about how you move your body, what facial expressions you pull, and how you gesticulate when speaking with people. Yet, those things tell other people a lot about you.

If you want to be in control of the impression you make, you need to be in control over your body.

Imagine this.

Someone walks into a room. Their shoulders are hunched. Their eyes are darting around the room. And they keep fiddling with their fingers.

This person is about to have a job interview.

What's the first impression their potential new boss will have?

That they are confident?

That they feel secure in themselves?

That they are nervous?

That they don't really want to be there?

Probably the last two statements, right?

But the person might simply have been thinking about an argument they had with their partner which they are still upset about.

The problem? The interviewer won't know that and might write them off at sight because they're looking for someone more confident.

The truth is, they might *be* nervous about the interview, but if they only learn to control their body, they'll *appear* less nervous. Chances are that once they control their body, they will *feel* less nervous.

That's the funny thing about body language—act confident and you start feeling confident. Act happy and you start feeling happy. Or at the very least—you feel happier or more confident than before.

Now, let's have a look at what you and others communicate using your bodies. This will help you decode what others are thinking and how you present yourself to people!

And once you become aware of what *you* are doing with your body, you can decide how you want to show up.

Just beware that nothing is written in stone—you have to look at a person's overall body language and figure out what's going on in their life before you can determine what they're truly thinking!

1) Walking and sitting with a straight back (good posture) implies confidence.
2) Keeping eye contact for much of a conversation (not all of it, it's not a staring competition!) shows confidence, honesty, and interest.

3) Leaning forward slightly when someone is speaking shows interest in what they are saying.

4) Tapping your fingers/feet or constantly changing your position implies nervousness, impatience, or unease.

5) Crossing your arms/legs shows you're not open to someone or to what they are saying, or you might simply be standing your ground.

6) Darting your eyes about communicates nervousness or guilt, as does looking down at the ground.

7) Staring into space or constantly looking away from someone might indicate that you're not paying attention.

8) Turning your palms up shows you have nothing to hide and/ or that you're open to what's being said.

9) Pinching your lips together shows you're unhappy or dissatisfied about something.

10) If you scrunch your nose, it signals disgust, while flaring your nostrils either signals getting ready to fight or an attraction to something or someone.

11) Putting your hands on your hips can be a sign that you feel in control or are preparing to stand your ground or fight.

12) Clenching your hands—whether together, or holding on to something tightly—can indicate you're nervous, trying to "get a hold of yourself," or that you are angry.

13) Tilting your head indicates you're thinking about something or considering what's being said.

14) A firm handshake signals confidence.

15) Raising your eyebrows indicates you're surprised or don't quite believe what you're hearing, seeing, or feeling.

16) Breathing fast or speaking at an unnaturally fast speed implies nervousness, stress, or unease of some form (or simply being winded whether from physical exercise or, in the case of the breathing, due to medical troubles such as asthma or heart disease!).

The interesting thing is that most of us don't consider what we communicate with our bodies. Yet, how people judge us and interpret what we're saying has everything to do with how we use our bodies.

Likewise, we interpret what people say depending on how they stand, their tone of voice, their facial expression, and so forth, but we're rarely conscious of it. In other words, we don't realize that this is what we're doing.

NOTE

People's "personal space"—i.e. their "bubble"—is the space they consider "theirs." It's different for everyone, and often depends on their personality or even their culture. If you've ever felt uncomfortable with someone standing too close to you, you know what it is. Probably you've stood very close to a lot of uncomfortable people in an elevator at one point or another.

When you sit or stand next to someone, respect their personal space or they might not enjoy interacting with you. In other words—don't stand or sit too close to them unless you know them well. You can still pat their hand, touch their shoulder, and so forth once they are comfortable being around you.

EXERCISE

Spend the next few days paying attention to how you're sitting, walking, and standing. Pay attention to what you do when you're speaking with someone. Also start paying attention to what other people are doing when they are talking to you.

To remind yourself to check in on what your body is doing, wear a bracelet or a ring. Every time you see it, you'll remember why you wore it in the first place.

Creating Connection Through Body Language

When you read the body language interpretation chart above, did you consider how body language can be used to create connection? Like how to make friends more easily?

Try doing the exercise below and see if people seem more open to chatting with you—particularly people you're meeting for the first time.

EXERCISE 1

When sitting down to have a conversation with someone new (i.e. someone who isn't a friend even if you already know *of* them), uncross your arms, legs, and hands. Lean forward slightly to listen to them speak. Look them in the eye for much of the conversation (apart from when contemplating something), but make sure you aren't staring—just be sure to meet their eye for the most part. Keep your body pretty still—don't constantly change your position, tap your fingers, etc. If you do this, you might just find people are more open with you!

There's something else you can do to create connection when interacting with people.

Have you ever noticed when speaking to someone that you copy what they are doing?

Yes, really—copy them!

Not like a parrot who repeats everything they say, but rather mimic some of their movements?

It's true. When we enjoy speaking with someone, we copy their body language. It's called matching and mirroring.

Sounds crazy?

Next time you have a conversation with someone you're interested in or you're attracted to, pay attention to your actions and you'll find that you will want to copy their movements.

This goes two ways—your friends will copy you, too! For example, if you put a finger to your chin, pondering something, you will find that they will do the same, or something similar, such as touching their cheek.

Interestingly, if you want to establish a connection with someone, you can start to match and mirror some of their body language *before* it happens naturally. You can't copy everything they do, but just mirror a few of their movements.

Let's say you really liked the speaker at an event. When the event is over, you go up to them and tell them you appreciate what they had to say. They are standing feet hip width apart (that confident speaker stance) and hands on their hips. So you position yourself opposite of them, standing in the same position, and when they move their hands, so do you.

Sounds complicated? It gets easier. Start by practicing with friends and family—chances are they won't notice, but in the beginning you might get distracted by trying to look at their body language and forget to listen to what they have to say!

EXERCISE 2

When having conversations with people, notice if you feel compelled to match and mirror their body language or if you find them copying you. If you meet someone for the first time, try to match some of their movements to see if they start to relax faster in your company. Also, try to watch other people when they talk to one another. Do they copy each other's body language?

Don't match and mirror *everything* someone does. That will come across as strange!

Do you remember the first exercise in this section—the one where you sit leaning slightly forward when talking to someone? Do that while also occasionally mirroring their body language and see what happens.

Using Body Language to Your Advantage

While it might be funny to see how you automatically hunch your back when you see a nasty teacher, flare your nostrils at someone attractive, or match and mirror your friend's body language, what good does it do you to know about these things? How can it help you succeed in life?

Let's get back to the job interview, only let's make it that *you* are the candidate for the job.

You walk into the interviewer's office.

Your back is straight. Your stride is confident. You look them straight in the eye, hold out your hand, and greet them with a smile and a firm handshake.

When you sit down in front of them, you keep your arms open and legs uncrossed, and you keep eye contact for much of the time when they speak. You lean forward slightly whenever they speak for any length of time. You make an effort to match and mirror some of their movements, and you smile and tilt your head to consider what they said when they ask you a difficult question.

By the time you walk out, chances are, you've made a good impression. (Assuming you answered their questions, and nicely!)

You'll make the same good impression if you go on a date and use the above body language. Again, of course, assuming you say nice things to your date! (More about words in a bit.)

If, on the other hand, you sit hunched over, keep looking anywhere but at the person's eyes, tap your fingers, cross your legs, and lean away from the other person, they are unlikely to think well of you. Especially if you pinch your mouth or scrunch your nose when they say things you disagree with.

Taking charge of your body is, to a large extent, taking charge of how others perceive you.

Think about that for a moment—if you learn to control your body language, you learn to control other people's impression of you.

You should still be you. You shouldn't change your personality. You just learn to use your body language to more clearly communicate things. We all have habits that we've become unconscious of, like tapping our feet when thinking, hunching our shoulders because we're used to sitting in a certain position when relaxing at home, and so forth. All those things might give people the wrong impression.

Plus, if you get nervous a lot and it comes out through your body language, people might fail to see *the real you.* The person underneath the nervousness.

Remember, the more you *act* confident, the more you *feel* confident!

TIPS

Smile at people. Smiles open doors because they show a) that you are happy and b) that you're happy to see the other person. You can make someone in the shop happy simply by smiling at them when you pay for your groceries. The more you smile, the happier people will become around you. Don't walk around smiling like a phony, but smile as much as you can when you have the opportunity to do so.

And here's another cool thing: your voice changes when you smile. That's why, when leaving a voice note, or speaking on the phone, you should smile. At least if you want the person on the other end of the line to receive the message well.

Using the Right Words in Conversations and Negotiations

Words are super important. After all, while studies suggest they only make up 10% of what we communicate to people, they make up 100% of the facts we share. They are what we use to share stories and anecdotes. Whether we mean what we say on the other hand, or how we are *feeling*, tends to come across in our body language.

Consider this: How can you argue that you should go to one college or another without using words? How can you convince your parents to let you go on a date without using words? How can you convince your boss to give you a raise without using words?

You can't. Whether the words are spoken, written, or communicated through sign language, you need them. Unless, of course, you act something out using mime or similar means, but in modern culture, that's unlikely.

The problem with words is that we're rarely taught *how* to use them.

Yeah, yeah, I know. You had an English test only the other day. But that doesn't mean you know *how to use words to communicate clearly and effectively*. So let's have a look at that next, shall we?

Let's say someone (such as a very irritating sibling) is sitting drumming on a metal bucket. It's making an awful racket. And eventually you snap. You turn to them and say something nasty.

What have you communicated?

That you're upset, right?

But you haven't said *why*. Nor have you expressed *what you'd like* to happen.

What's more, do you think saying something nasty will get you the desired result?

Let's say instead that you said, "That noise is really getting to me and I can't concentrate on what I'm doing. It's really important I complete this work or I will fail my English exam. Would you mind stopping, or perhaps going to another room and doing it there? I'd really appreciate it."

If you express yourself that way (but using whatever words work for you, not perhaps the "stuffy" language I've used here), you're not taking out your annoyance on your sibling (which likely will only lead to them drumming louder as they're now angry with you).

Instead, you're communicating how their action *is making you feel* without implying that that's what *they* want you to feel. They might not be doing it to upset you—perhaps they are feeling agitated and it's coming out in the drumming. Or they are daydreaming and are completely unaware of drumming. Or they really want to annoy you. Then, don't let them— usually they stop by themselves if you don't get irritated!

Here's the thing. If they want your attention and you give it to them when they act out, then they are going to *keep* acting out.

Try to give them positive attention instead. Acknowledge them, ask them about their day, play with them, hug them, and then ask politely when you need time to yourself. Chances are that if they feel they've already gotten attention, they'll leave you alone when you need it. (Review the tips on building great relationships in chapter 3.)

You have also, perhaps most importantly, communicated *what it is you want*. You want them to stop drumming or go somewhere else and drum where it won't disturb you.

Can you see that if you express yourself in this way, your sibling is much less likely to get angry with you and *much more likely to do as you ask*? If you usually scream at them and get upset, it might take them a while to adjust to your new way of communicating, but if you keep doing it, chances are they'll become more agreeable to your wishes.

Let's imagine another scenario.

Your parent asks you to pack away your iPad and go to bed. But it's Friday night, and you think you should be allowed to stay up as long as you like. So you simply look up and glare at them.

Through that glare, you have communicated that you're unhappy about the situation.

But not *why*.

Nor have you acknowledged that you understand why there is a set bedtime or why your parents do their best to enforce it.

You did not say the following in a nice tone of voice: "It's Friday, therefore, I feel it's unfair that I have to go to bed at ten as I don't have school tomorrow. Perhaps we could extend it till eleven? Please. I'd really appreciate it as I enjoy getting to relax on a Friday night, as I have so many extracurricular activities during the week. Coming home and doing nothing on a Friday night feels like a treat. Please."

Now that expresses *why* you want to stay up late. What's more, you're showing your parents *respect* by being nice and polite while asking. They're much more likely to give in to your demands if you show respect for them. Plus, you didn't ask to stay up all night—instead you were reasonable in your demands.

If this doesn't work, you could take it further by negotiating the terms, i.e. throwing in an "if you do x for me, I'll do y for you."

"It's Friday, therefore, I feel it's unfair that I have to go to bed at ten as I don't have school tomorrow. I understand that upsetting my sleep routine too much isn't healthy, but a little bit surely can't hurt? How about you let me stay up an extra hour *if* I promise to be in bed on time throughout the school week *and* get up every morning without complaint? I'd really appreciate it as I enjoy getting to relax on a Friday night, as I have so many extracurricular activities during the week. Please."

Of course, that only works if you have problems going to bed and getting up during the week. It also only works if you honor your promises. Otherwise, next week, you're back to ten o'clock.

You could also suggest staying up an hour longer *if* you read a book for the last half hour (if your parents want you to read more).

Your parents might try to negotiate the terms, too.

Perhaps they'll say it's fine to stay up an extra half an hour (not an hour).

So why will the above work better than just getting upset and telling them it's unfair?

It works better because

    a)   You asked in a nice and respectful manner

    b)   You explained *why* you'd like that extra hour

    c)   You acknowledged that your parents care for you and that's *why* they have a set time for your bedtime (and you understand the importance of a good sleep routine)

    d)   You showed a willingness to obey their rules during the week *without* sulking

Effective communication leaves little to the imagination. You have to spell it out.

> Let's say it's a different scenario—you're negotiating something else. Here are the important components:
>
> 1) State what you want as clearly as possible
> 2) Ask for it in a nice and respectful manner
> 3) State *why* you deserve it or need it (depending on the situation)
> 4) If the other person is already doing something for you, acknowledge it/their efforts
> 5) Possibly, if appropriate, offer something in return

If you're negotiating a raise, it could be something like this:

"You've done a lot for me, Mrs. Dawson. You hired me straight out of school and have taught me a lot of things. What's more, you have truly offered me a nice place to work, and I've had the pleasure of watching this company grow. My family has also grown, and as I have been with you for some time now, and increased my sales numbers, I was hoping that a raise is possible. I really need it to be able to pay our bills. I will continue to work as hard as possible and attend as many sales workshops as I can to increase my numbers even more." (You can change the language to how *you* speak, but you get the gist of the *elements* you need to communicate.)

Here, you've outlined what Mrs. Dawson has done for you, you've explained why you deserve it and need it—a larger family—and you're offering to continue your hard work and find new ways to increase sales. And it's all been done in a very nice manner. As opposed to stomping your foot, saying you deserve a raise because you've worked darn hard for over two years and you're just not getting enough money now that you have a child. With that attitude, chances are, you won't get a raise.

But it doesn't stop here.

Remember that 90% of communication is non-verbal. You can tell someone what you want, but if you do so without showing in your tone of voice that you mean what you say, they won't take you seriously.

The expression on your face, your tone of voice, where your eyes are looking, and how you hold your body all communicate their own story.

Imagine this. Say you have a ten-year-old brother who is being told by your parents/guardians to go clean his bedroom. He shouts, "Fine, I'll do it." Then, he stomps off to his bedroom, slams the door, and you can hear him throwing things around as he cleans. After a while, he reappears and says sulkily to your parents, "I cleaned. Now give me my pocket money."

Imagine instead, if he happily goes to clean his room, then comes out and says, "I've cleaned now. It was really boring, but the room feels much nicer to be in. And I get that I should care for my things so that they last longer. Thanks for teaching me that. And thanks for taking care of cleaning the rest of the house—that's a massive job. You're awesome for doing it. Can I please have my pocket money now?"

Which version of your brother would you prefer?

Which version of your brother would you be likely to give bonus pocket money to?

Your parents might also fall into communication traps. They've had a long day. They're tired after work. They come home. Now they need to cook. Then clean. Then make sure you get to bed.

So instead of saying, "Please go do your homework if you haven't already. It's really important that you pass the next few tests if you want to get into your college of choice. And I really want that for you, because I want you to have a future that will make you happy," they might say, in an irritated voice, "Haven't you done your homework yet? How many times do I have to tell you? If you continue like this, you will make a mess of your future."

Now, in both instances, your parent is saying what they are saying because they love you and want you to have the life of your dreams.

However, in the second example, they are letting their frustration get the better of them. They've worked so hard to save money for your college fund. They are tired after a long day. And now you're not doing your part. Why do they have to keep reminding you—they've already told you a thousand times! It makes their life even harder if you don't do your part and, worse yet, if you *sulk* about doing your part.

When we look more closely at how we communicate, we also learn to see why others communicate the way they do. We learn to figure out what's really going on inside their head.

The Art of Saying "Please" and "Thank You"

Please and thank you get you far in life.

Remembering to thank someone for something they did for you, or simply thanking them for taking the time to speak with you, makes them more likely to give more of their time or do you more favors.

Being polite and using words like please and thank you, as well as wishing people a good day (or a fab, fantastic, awesome, lovely, or great day), will make them like you better.

Why?

Because they'll feel like you *care*. What's more, it shows you have respect for them.

When my little one or teens say, "Give me the iPad," I don't hand it over.

If they say, "Please can you give me the iPad?" on the other hand, I feel compelled to do it. They're being nice, so I want to be nice in return.

In fact, I just messaged one of my teens to say what time I'll come pick her up, ending it with a hug emoji and asking whether she'd want to get picked up at location x or location y. Her response? "Location y." Not a "thank you." Or a "please." Or a heart emoji. Or any other form of gratitude.

My irritation levels? Shooting through the roof. I don't want to spend my time driving to pick up someone who isn't showing any gratitude for my kindness.

Of course, words are only a small part of communication (unless it's the written word). When you say please, thank you, or anything else to show respect or gratitude, you have to remember to look people in the eye, smile, and be sincere. If your tone of voice is that of a sulky three-year-old, chances are no one will find you polite. And if you shuffle your feet and look at the floor, they'll think you're either super shy or you're being nice to them against your will.

You can think of body language like emojis. If you're asking someone for a favor and sending an angry emoji, they're not very likely to respond.

You need to show love through your body language! Not by hugging or kissing, but simply by being genuine and happy and/or grateful.

A tip is to simply learn to be grateful for what people do for you. Consider their time and effort. Show your gratitude through the pleases and thank yous.

But what if someone is rude? I don't mean rude as in saying something nasty, but simply rude as in not being polite or friendly.

What do you do then?

Well, I tend to refer to people like that as "sourkrauts" and grapefruits. Then I challenge myself to be the person I want to be when around them. If they are rude, so be it, but I'm not going to sink to their level. I want to be proud of who I am.

Basically, I continue to be a sunbeam in the face of their rudeness and don't let their sour ways dampen my day! Sometimes, that even leads to them eventually giving in and smiling back!

Other times they don't, but at least you know you're still being the person who you want to be. There's no point getting irritated and walking away feeling like a sourkraut yourself!

Checking In—Expressing Genuine Interest in Others

If someone greets you with a big cheery, "Goooood morning! How are you? You look more rested after the weekend!" chances are you'll feel pretty good about them. You might even stop and chat.

Basically, they're being friendly, so you respond in kind. What's more, they've just shown they care: 1) They are asking how you are, meaning they care to find out. 2) They show they've paid attention, telling you that you look more well rested after the weekend.

Now, how do you think they'll feel if at the end of your chat with them, you say, "Have an epic day!"? They'll probably feel better than if you just walk off, right?

You might prefer saying something like, "Stay blessed," or, "Take care!" What matters is that you show you care about them by wishing them a good day, one way or another.

It's easy enough to say these things, and it can make someone's day. You never know when someone needs a bit of an "oomph" to help them along!

Now, wishing someone a good day is all well and good, but you have got to *mean* it.

When you say something, you have to mean it. When you ask a question, you have to honestly want to know the answer. When you wish someone well, it has to come from the heart. Otherwise, the conversation is insincere.

You know, like the shop assistants that look half dead at the end of their shift but still ask you how you're doing when you buy something. You can tell from a mile away they don't really want to know how you're doing. They're on autopilot, going through the motions, nothing more.

The last thing you want is for people to think you're insincere, or simply don't care.

So when you're talking to someone, *think about what you're saying.* Don't ask someone how they're doing if you don't want to find out. Don't wish someone a good day unless you truly mean it.

Likewise, when someone is speaking with you, are you truly listening?

Or are you perhaps busy wondering what they are *really* thinking about you? Or maybe you're thinking about what you will do when the conversation is over? Or just what you're going to say next?

You could also be busy judging them for what they have to say, or you could be ten miles away, daydreaming about something else entirely.

When you truly listen to someone, you're looking at their body language *and* hearing what they are saying. You're gauging, not just what they are saying, but how they feel about it.

Just by doing those two things (listening and looking), you become present to the moment and the person right in front of you.

As humans, we have a habit of referring everything back to ourselves. When someone chats about their friend, we think of our friend. When they talk about their troubles, we think about our troubles.

We rarely stop to consider the other person's experience (which is different from how we would have experienced it) and show true empathy.

Here's a tip: Get curious! Try to step into how the other person is thinking and feeling (not about you, but about what they're speaking about!). The more curious you get about others, the easier it is to become present and truly hear what they're saying!

EXERCISE

When you're chatting with someone and they are explaining something or telling you a story, check where your mind goes off to. Are you thinking about what to say next, judging them, or doing something else that isn't truly listening? Or are you truly present and hearing what they are saying?

If you're curious to learn more, you can also look up "active listening" online! It's a technique people use to become great conversationalists . . . because one of the main things you need to be a good conversationalist is listening skills!

Mind Reading Online and Offline

As we are communicating so much more online and through texts these days, it's super important to be clear.

Remember the example I gave about my teen responding to a message earlier? I told her what time I would pick her up and asked where. She responded with the location, nothing else. No "please," "thank you," or a nice emoji. I was left thinking she was rude and why should I spend my time driving her to and from places if she does not appreciate it?

What I'm doing is called a mindread. I'm interpreting her emotions based on her message.

As there was no gratitude in her message, I interpreted it as her being ungrateful.

So was she ungrateful, or was I making it up? After all, she didn't say she was ungrateful, she just didn't express any gratitude.

In real life, you have body language to guide you as to what people are thinking and feeling, but online, you only have words. So you have to be clearer than ever in what you say to ensure the message gets across.

You also have to stop yourself from misinterpreting things when reading other people's messages.

Unfortunately, in real life, we often interpret things wrongly, too.

"My partner often comes home late, *therefore* they are cheating." (Your partner is planning a surprise birthday for you and has been out shopping and arranging things with your friends for the past couple of weeks.)

"My friend chose to go with Alex to a soccer game instead of me, *therefore* she prefers Alex to me." (Your friend's dad pointed out that she hasn't spent enough time with Alex lately and should bring Alex along to the game.)

"My girlfriend seems down lately, *therefore* she is unhappy with our relationship." (Your girlfriend is having issues at school and feels insecure. Her school troubles mean she suddenly thinks you might not like her as she can't be worthy of you if she can't even get her stupid grades right.)

"My mother snaps a lot, *therefore* she doesn't like me." (She's stressed at work, and by the time she gets home, she wants to sit down and not move. Any loud noise or argument feels like a bomb going off in her head.)

Look, while body language might alert you to the fact that something doesn't add up (your partner says they're happy, but clearly they aren't as they look miserable all the time), you have to stop yourself from weaving meaning into it.

If someone says or does something that makes you think something's up, then ask them about it instead of acting on how you feel.

If your partner looks miserable all the time, ask them about it. If they say, "No, everything's fine," you have to assess if that could be true, or you could say, "Look, you seem really down. If everything's fine, why are you suddenly so sad? Or maybe not sad, but you look sort of . . . I don't know, just not happy anymore. Maybe you don't want to talk about it, but can you at least let me know if it's because of me or our relationship?"

Sometimes, how other people act makes *us* feel something. Like in the example above—suddenly your partner comes home late all the time. Why? Could they be cheating on you?

Perhaps you spend a lot of time thinking about this, getting more and more upset, until you burst and shout at your partner, "I know you're cheating on me, you always come home late."

You *made something up* about them being late and now you're acting on it *even if you don't know if it's true.*

Imagine instead that you said, "Look, I know this is probably just me, but I've been worried lately. I see so little of you. Are you still happy with me? Are we still fine?" If they say yes, tell them you'd love to find a way to spend more time together. If they have to work late, perhaps you can see more of them on the weekend?

In the example I shared about my teen not saying "please" and "thank you" when I offered to pick her up, instead of messaging her back saying she's so rude for not thanking me, I could say, "Hey, I don't think you meant to be rude, but if you respond like that, I feel like you don't have any gratitude for what I do. Could you perhaps try to say 'please' or 'thank you' in the future?"

She might not even have *meant* to be rude. For all I know, she could have been completely distracted when writing the message.

As it turned out, she was on someone else's phone and in a hurry.

How do I know this? Because I asked her about it. I want her to learn to show gratitude, and I shared with her that I was working on this book and using her message as an example. We had a nice chat about it.

While on the topic of mindreads, let's talk about flirting. Because when people flirt, they tend to do a lot of mindreading.

Some men and women are naturally flirtatious. They compliment you. They touch your arm while speaking. They constantly smile at you. They call you "babe," "honey," or whatever term happens to be popular right now, and they do it without it feeling sleazy. Like it just sounds right when they say it. When they write texts, they use a lot of "..." "Let's meet later..." As if something exciting will happen later...

In some cases, it means they are flirting with you. In other instances...it means that's just the way they are.

The easiest way to find out what anyone's *implying* (but not saying out loud)? Ask them.

If your friends are spending less time with you, ask them why, or ask them if they want to spend more time with you.

Don't make up assumptions in your head about why people are doing what they're doing—if you don't know, ask.

And the next time your mother or friend snaps at you, consider if it's because they don't love you or because they're tired, hungry, or irritated. That doesn't give them the right to snap, but it's perhaps the *reason* why they do it. Ask them.

We all have good days and bad days, but the more we start to pay attention to how we interact with others, the better we get at showing we genuinely care . . . even on days when we feel like we've been through a hurricane (and would like to hit something because we're so upset)!

An easy thing to do? On days when you don't feel like being happy around others, tell them why. "I'm tired today, so don't take it the wrong way if I'm not paying as much attention as usual."

Remember: you communicate all the time—through words, actions, and body language. So use it to your advantage!

6

Writing Messages Like a Pro

How to pen great messages

Now, this is one of those topics that probably sounds boring, but like all communication, if you learn how to do it well, it will take you places. If nothing else, you'll have a lot better relationships with the people around you!

That includes your bosses, friends, neighbors, family, colleagues, employees, heck, even the people who service your car and book you in at the dentist. The better you get at communicating, the better those people will treat you . . . most of the time.

There are always the sourkrauts . . .

We've covered most of the important stuff in the communication chapter already, so we just need to turn it into writing more specifically. You do remember what we covered about saying "please" and "thank you," wishing people a good day, and being overall polite and clear in your communication, don't you?

If not, here's a breakdown:

- Always be genuine (mean what you say and say what you mean)
- Spell things out clearly and when other people speak, if they don't spell it out clearly, ask (don't make assumptions)
- Try to say something nice in every conversation
- Truly listen when others speak—take in their words and body language

That's it! Pretty simple, isn't it?

Now, below, I've chosen to use the word "email" as a lot of more formal communication still happens over email.

That said, many schools and workplaces use internal messaging systems, and you're communicating with friends, parents, and others through whatever platform they're using. I've just used the term "email" as those messages are usually longer, more structured, and more formal than the messages you send to your family over some other messaging app.

NOTE

As you communicate online, you'll be connected to people not just in your area but all over the world. So here's a reminder: always be kind. Some of the people you might message grew up speaking a different language, so it's important to be respectful and to be careful not to judge others by how they write.

Tone of Voice

Your tone of voice when writing a message will vary depending on who you are messaging.

With tone of voice, I mean: "Yo, What's going down?" as opposed to "Hello, how are you, Mrs. Robinson?" One (the first) is informal, while the other (the second) is formal.

If you don't know someone, you're better off being formal than informal. Work emails, emails to teachers, and so forth are usually formal.

That said, if you work with someone closely, you usually become more and more informal the better you get to know them. Still, you might not want to cross certain lines (such as writing "Yo, Dude, waz up?").

That said, you know best how the people in your life communicate. Some industries and people are very formal, others aren't.

I have business emails I sign off with "xx" because in London, that was pretty common if you got to know the person you did business with.

However, I wouldn't do that when emailing local politicians . . . unless I know them. It has happened that I've started emails to politicians with "Hello darling . . ." But that's not what you'd generally do . . . and if you live in America, you probably wouldn't say "darling" at all.

Lastly, whether you're emailing your boss, your co-worker, your mom, your partner, or someone else, keep in mind that people respond well to positivity and enthusiasm.

It's the same as the please and thank you—the nicer and happier you come across, the better response you usually get.

For example, let's say your parents aren't living together and you spend alternate weeks at their homes.

Hi Mom,

I hope you had a great week.

What time will you get home on Friday? So I know when I can come over. :)

I really look forward to seeing you, Mom! :) *(Here you show enthusiasm at seeing your mom again.)*

Love,

Maria

Xoxox

Want something even shorter for a text?

Hi Mom, can't wait to see you Friday! :) What time can I come around? Xoxo

---

Compare that to receiving a text that says:

What time can I come on Friday?

In the first example, you are likely to make your mom happy. In the second, you aren't. How she responds might also vary depending on which text you choose to send. People who feel appreciated, loved, and valued are much more likely to respond with the same.

Want something meatier for an email or longer message?

Hi Mom,

I hope you had a great week. Did you go to the dentist? I hope your tooth was fixed and is no longer giving you problems! (*Here, you show you care by asking questions about your mom's life.*)

My week was filled with exams … a bit stressful … and boring (I know, it's good to learn and it will get me into college, but not ALL topics are fun!). Still I think I did alright :D (*Here you show a bit of your life … it's nice for your parents to understand what's happening.*)

What time will you get home on Friday? So I know when I can come over.

I really look forward to seeing you, Mom! :) (*Here you show enthusiasm at seeing your mom again.*)

Your loving, wonderful, and utterly amazing daughter, (*Here, you're having a bit of fun.*)

Maria

Xoxox

Saying the same but in less words?

Hi Mom,

I look forward to seeing you Friday. What time should we make it? By the way, how did your job interview go? I have been wondering about that! :) I hope it went well, or if it's not for you, that you find something much better soon! I did alright on my tests. :)

Hugs,

Maria

The Skeleton of an Email or Message

There is a structure that's pretty common when you write formal or semi-formal emails and messages. The "skeleton" of the message, if you so like. It tends to be fairly similar no matter who you're messaging.

When you write a formal or semi-formal message, you usually structure it a little something like this:

Hello [insert name],

How are you? I hope well!

[insert purpose of email/message such as asking when you will get your car back from the mechanic]

Thank you so much!

Have a fantastic day further.

Kind regards,

Maria

> Hello [insert name],
>
> How are you? I hope you're staying dry in this downpour … what crazy weather we're having! (*As you can see, this is a bit more chatty and you can insert your own version, such as saying "It was lovely speaking with you last Saturday. I hope you made it home alright after the event! Following up on what we were discussing … "*)
>
> [insert purpose of email/message such as asking when you will get your car back from the mechanic]
>
> Thank you kindly for your time.
>
> Have a wonderful weekend.
>
> Warm regards,
>
> Maria

Remember to be clear (spell things out) and always say "please" and "thank you." If appropriate, ask how someone is doing, and wish them a good (lovely, fantastic, fab, tremendously wonderful, incredible, amazing, awesome, fabulous, nice, great—take your pick) morning/day/evening/ night/week/weekend.

Of course, if it's someone who is "stuffy" (i.e. very formal), do *not* wish them "a tremendously wonderful" or "freakin' fantastic" day. That kind of fabulously amazing wish you have to save for people whom you know *and* you're positive would appreciate that kind of wording. Stick to "Have a great day!" if you're unsure.

Apart from being *clear* and spelling out *exactly* what you are thinking when messaging friends and family, there isn't really a formula for how you write the message. Just remember the above example where someone asks when s/he can come over to his/her mom's place. You want to be nice, polite, kind, and enthusiastic (about the person you are emailing, or whatever you're talking about in the email) wherever possible. And hey, by asking people questions and taking an interest in what's happening in their lives, you show you care. People tend to appreciate that.

Typos, Spell-Check, and Other Interesting Things

Autocorrect has led to millions of hilarious emails and texts being sent across the globe.

Those typos and autocorrects are usually funny when we look back at them later, but when we've just emailed our boss something really, really weird, it's not so funny . . . unless your boss has a really good sense of humor!

I actually once got a friend of mine to help me with some sales/marketing ideas to send someone I was doing an internship with. My friend edited my ideas, sent them back to me, and I sent them to my boss.

Only later did I realize that my friend had added a title under my name (Maria, Head of xxxxxxxxx). And what he made me out to be was . . . perhaps funny for him and me, but not for my boss. It was extremely rude. My boss took it well, saying it would teach me a lesson never to forward anything again without reading to the end or double-checking everything.

Not using spell-check has led to as many hilarious emails and texts as using autocorrect and not reading through the messages before sending. Plus, whether you're writing an email or a post on Facebook, people might look down on you if they see too many typos. After all, there's spell-check. Why aren't you using it?

People make snap decisions.

"If someone can't spell, they're stupid." That's not true. Of course not.

But it's a well-known secret that dating profiles filled with typos will be glossed over. Meaning, when people see a profile filled with spelling mistakes, they swipe left more often.

Why?

Because, either the person isn't the smartest cookie in the cookie jar or they didn't care enough about their profile to make it free of spelling errors. And if the latter is the case, how much do they *really* care about meeting someone?

Look, making snap decisions is often bad for many reasons, but we all do it. We don't even realize we do it. So if you're sending out emails/ messages, look them through before you hit send unless you want the receiver to judge you for any errors.

The thing is, we aren't even aware of making snap decisions sometimes (Malcolm Gladwell's *Blink* is really good if you wanna learn more about that). Just imagine someone showed you a photo of a dark alley at night where the houses look a bit worn down, dilapidated. Would you say it looks safe to hang out there at night?

Probably not. That doesn't *mean* it's not safe, but based on what you've heard about dark alleys at night, you make a snap decision.

We have to make snap decisions all the time, otherwise we'd spend our whole lives trying to make decisions and still make the wrong ones.

And remember what I spoke about in the communication chapter? How we weave meaning into things? It's kind of the same thing—we have a few facts and based on those facts, we paint a picture. But perhaps we don't have *enough* facts to really paint that picture.

It's the same when we read messages from people. We tend to *immediately* make a snap decision about what the message means. The problem is that often we read between the lines and sometimes we weave the wrong meaning into it.

Why?

Because we don't have all the facts.

A dark alley with some old houses isn't always dangerous—for all we know, it could be an alley in the safest city in the world . . . or even a movie set. We just don't have enough facts to make a decision . . . but we still do.

So when someone texts you to say they have to cancel and can't hang out with you, it means just that—they have to cancel and can't hang out with you.

It doesn't mean they don't care about you or likes some other friend more . . . Or maybe it does, but you don't know that.

This is why it's so important to be clear in your communication—otherwise, people will make up things about you and what you say that aren't true. They will *interpret* your words and actions.

So next time you cancel on a friend whom you don't want to cancel on, say so.

"Sorry, I have to cancel our meeting today. I was really looking forward to seeing you, but Mom has to run an errand and I have to babysit my sister. I love my sister, but this stinks :(Can we reschedule?"

Or you could try: "I can't see you today, something's come up that I can't get out of. Can we please reschedule? Soon? Like even tomorrow if you have time :)"

Obviously, use your own words, but convey that you really did not want to cancel and that you want to see them soon. That way, they won't think you're just making up excuses not to see them.

7

Social Media Skills, Thrills, and Threats

Surviving in the online jungle

Let's start with the good news: Social media is fantastic.

You can reconnect with people you haven't seen for years. You can stay in touch with people who live in different locations from you. You can meet new people whom you otherwise wouldn't have met. You can build a following in a specific niche (such as painting, tailoring, fashion, carpentry, plumbing, poetry, skating, etc.) and even become an influencer who *earns money* from social media.

The bad news?

Anything you say can and will be used against you. Such as your next boss checking your public feed and realizing you're cracking jokes about how boring it is to have to go to work.

Yeah, that.

Also, anything you say and any image you share can be screenshotted and shared with people you are not friends with. This can get awkward if you're having an argument with your boy/girlfriend and they decide to screenshot it and share it. Or if you ask someone out via a message on social media and they screenshot it and share it.

If you want to have a private conversation with someone, don't have it on social media. Meet face-to-face or give them a call. Yes, they can record a conversation but who does that? They'd be written off as a bit weird. But that inbox of theirs will always be there. They might scroll through old messages at any time (such as when they are really angry with you) and do something stupid, such as screenshotting them and sharing them.

(Note to you, the reader: never screenshot and share people's messages. It's a huge invasion of privacy, and you might end up getting sued in the absolute worst-case scenario.)

If there is something you feel you can share, but just with a select few (such as your funny jokes about how boring work is), then ensure your post privacy is set properly. In other words, make sure the posts aren't public so that future employers won't be able to see them.

TIPS

Always think of social media as a platform for sharing things. If you don't want your message to be shared, don't post it.

Staying Safe Online

First things first—safety.

If you make friends outside your actual social circle on social media, consider that people can find you (and stalk you) if you have pictures that show where you live, work, or go to school.

If you have an open (i.e. public) profile that shows your home and when you're going on vacation, well, a thief might just have found their golden opportunity.

Here's the thing though, on most sites now, you can control *who* sees what posts. You can make some posts public, others can be shown to your connections/friends only, yet others can be shown to specific lists only.

The point? Don't show pictures or write about where you go to school, live, or work and make it public unless you're comfortable with anyone knowing those details. And definitely don't make it public when you're going on vacation unless you have good security where you live!

Go to your privacy settings and have a look around to figure out how to control who sees what, if you haven't already. You can also use YouTube to look up how privacy settings work for different platforms.

I could warn you and say that connecting with people online and then meeting up with them is dangerous. It can be. But the truth is, that's how the world works today. I've traveled the world and met lots of people online that I have gotten to know in real life. And before the Internet was something everyone used (yeah, imagine that), I had a pen pal from Kenya whom I later met up with in real life. We're still friends today.

For many centuries, people have connected through letters before meeting up in real life. In other words—chatting before you meet up in real life is nothing new!

Today you can use apps to meet not just dates, but friends and business associates, which can be extremely useful. Especially if you move to a new city and want to make new friends or find your next business partner. However, some stories have ended badly, and that's why you need to be *careful*. Don't take risks. Be smart about it.

Here are some tips if you chat with strangers online (beyond thanking them for their likes on your Instagram post—in other words, strangers whom you have deeper conversations with as you'd like to get to know them and possibly meet up with them).

First of all, get on a video call ASAP to see if they look like they say they do.

If they look like their photos, fantastic. At least you know they're not a fifty-year-old pretending to be nineteen. BUT remember that they can have a side of their personality in real life that does not come through online.

For example, you won't notice if someone gets really angry for nothing and starts swearing and hitting things whenever they are upset by chatting with them online. Likewise, you won't discover if they're the kind of person who always makes you chicken soup when you're sick or helps old ladies and gentlemen cross the street.

Secondly, make sure to meet them before sharing anything you wouldn't want to be made public. Remember, whatever you say can be screenshotted and used. Even if you're speaking with them over the phone, they can tell others what you have said and start rumors. Most people are nice and won't do that, but before you meet someone a couple of times in real life, use caution.

Lastly, if you decide to meet with someone, meet them in a public place together with your friends or parents. If you don't bring your parents, make sure they know what you're doing and where you are. Always choose a public meeting place, at least for the first couple of times you meet up. You don't get to know someone in an hour—it takes time. So don't rush a friendship. Or as I say when giving dating advice: You can fall in love on the first date, but most people who do so are out of love by the tenth date. So don't act on your feelings right away. Take your time to figure out if they will last first.

If you're under a certain age, meeting people on social media might not be the best idea (in fact, I wouldn't recommend it). But let's say you have a YouTube channel about trains. You connect with another kid who has a YouTube channel about trains. You want to meet up. That's nice. Talk to your parents about it, and let them help you set up a supervised meeting.

If, on the other hand, you're fifteen and a twenty-year-old whom you don't know starts hitting on you online, then warning bells should go off. Likewise, if an adult starts paying you attention online, tell your parents.

Furthermore, never ever give people money online unless they're doing an official fundraising campaign on a place like GoFundMe or Indiegogo or something like that. And NEVER hand out your debit or credit card details (or your ID for that matter) to ANYONE. Don't even put them in an email to your parents because your email can get hacked!

And that's the last thing to remember—even if you only chat with people you trust online, your account can get hacked. Use long, complicated passwords that contain both letters, numbers, and some funky symbols when you create accounts. And when using a browser, check the settings to prevent trackers (Safari is good with this). There are special browser extensions, apps, and other tools online you can look into as well if you want to be extra safe!

Set aside time in the weekend or one evening to sit down with your parents, or by yourself, and go through some YouTube videos on online safety for different platforms and when using a browser. Then install whatever browser extensions you want, or simply check your privacy settings. Do the same with your social media accounts.

While on the topic of safety—don't click on links to pages you're unsure about, and don't buy through vendors you aren't sure about. A store might look legit, but that doesn't mean it is. Do your research before forking out your card to buy something.

Remember: Never share your address (home, school, work), ID, or credit card details with strangers. Check your privacy settings. If you don't know how to control what content gets seen by whom, look through YouTube to find instruction videos. And if you meet someone online, try to verify they're "real" by getting on a video call if you want to get to know them better than just commenting on posts. If you meet them in real life, tell your family where you are going and meet in a public place.

Your Online Persona

Let's say you're building a following online. You want to become a TikTok/YouTube/Instagram/AnyOtherSite influencer. Great. Fantastic. You might get rich. But before you get started, consider this: What is the message you want to give others? Maybe you just want to show off cool fashion and help others with their style. Wonderful.

But what message are you giving them? You can show people fashion and be a real diva about it, or you can encourage people to find their individual style and help them feel beautiful. In themselves. No matter what looks they were born with or size of wallet they have.

Whenever you share something, you have the opportunity to uplift others.
So instead of worrying about the amount of likes you're getting, worry about how people feel when they see your posts.

Ah, and here is the social media downfall: ego.

When you get a like, you get a rush of chemicals to your brain. Yep. Weird as that might sound, you get a rush of "happy chemicals." You feel good.

Which is why it's so easy to get addicted to social media.

And if you don't get likes . . . your ego might take a hit. What's wrong with my posts? What's wrong with me?

Perhaps you do need to improve the quality of the images, jokes, videos, or messages you share. Perhaps you need a class on how to create great social media posts. Those are available all over—get your parents to help you pick one if you're serious about learning. You can also start by simply checking out videos about it on YouTube.

Likewise, if you want to become an influencer, taking a course in people skills can be a good idea. Or communication skills. After all, you'll be talking to a lot of people. And to be heard and understood, people and communication skills will be vital.

That said, not everyone is destined to become a social media star.

Think of it this way: There are lots of comedians, but not everyone is as popular as Trevor Noah. They don't have the right mass appeal.

What do I mean by that? They don't appeal to *everyone*. Trevor is good at jokes that entertain a lot of people. Not everyone is. That's fine.

Plus, there's a lot more to it than that. Becoming "famous" online requires nailing the right posting algorithm and, sometimes, it comes down to luck—some big star reposts what you've said and boom—you're famous.

As an offline comedian, it requires having an agent that books shows for you, arranges for PR, and so forth.

I have a friend who makes his living as a comedian, but chances are you don't know his name. Yet, he's still making a living out of it. He's still having fun.

You don't have to be the biggest influencer to have fun with social media.

Enjoying your life and having fun creating posts is a lot more important than having a big following.

Think of it this way—some people become actors because they want to become famous. Others become actors because they enjoy acting, and every time they act, they have a lot of fun. The person trying to get famous might think they'll only have fun once they get famous.

The weird thing? Most actors who get famous realize they didn't become any happier. Which, ironically, makes them depressed.

You get fulfillment from doing what you love, not having other people praise you for it.

That doesn't mean you shouldn't do your best to build an online following. Just don't get upset if it a) takes work, like learning how to create good posts, when to post, etc. or b) you don't get a massively large following.

Who knows—even if you only get 1,000 followers, one of them could be your next boss, friend, partner . . . Connections are super important—they are what build our lives, so work on them!

Social media is great in that you can connect with people outside your own circle and build a network.

Growing up in a small community where I was anything but popular and then attending high school in the city and instantly making friends, I can attest to the fact that sometimes you need to meet people *outside* your current circle to thrive. Just be careful, always chat with your parents, guardians, epic neighbors, marvelous grandparents, or other reliable  adults about it. No matter how old and wise we get, it's good to have others talk to us about our decisions. Even at the ripe age of (you don't even wanna know), I tell someone else where I go if I meet someone I've only met online.

Managing Your Time on Social Media Wisely

Whether you want to become an influencer or just use social media to catch up with people, schedule your social media time.

Why? Surely you can just chat with people whenever.

Well . . .

If you constantly have your phone on and stop to answer messages throughout the day, your thoughts are constantly interrupted. You aren't *truly* concentrating on anything. And that's a bit of a problem because then that becomes a pattern for your brain. You will find it harder and harder to concentrate even without your phone on.

Plus, everything else you're trying to do (like the boring stuff such as homework and cleaning) will take ten times longer if every two minutes you stop to check your phone or tablet. Put it away. Enjoy how your brain feels when you concentrate. And get stuff done at super speed! Then you can relax and enjoy social media when the important stuff is done.

What's more, unless you schedule your social media time, you might just find yourself aimlessly scrolling through posts. Before you know it, half an hour, or even more, has gone by.

If you're looking on YouTube to try to figure out your biology assessment or you're figuring out how to create that one epic hairstyle, fair enough. But endless scrolling does not accomplish anything. You'll just see a bunch of videos that teach you nothing (and aren't really entertaining, either) or posts that are completely meaningless.

You want to use your social media time to connect with cool people and learn cool things—decide up front what you're going to do once you get online and stick to it.

In short, *schedule your social media time*. And if you have a hard time sticking to the schedule, be wise about it. "I'll be on TikTok or Facebook for ten minutes when I come home from school." Right. Only that turned into fifty minutes.

But if you schedule the time *just* before dinner, you can't not put your phone down. You have to come to the table and eat.

You can also schedule social media time just before the school bus leaves in the morning or just before getting ready for bed at night. At least if you have a parent who removes your phone when you go to sleep so you won't spend the whole night scrolling . . .

It's the same with Netflix or anything else that might have you "accidentally" spending three hours binge-watching something.

I like to schedule things as rewards. Such as checking my messages *after* I've performed a certain task or spent x amount of hours working.

If you find it hard to concentrate in general (and that's why you reach for your phone), look up tips for concentration. You might want to talk to your parents about testing for ADD/ADHD as well. Yes, it is sometimes over-diagnosed, but raising a child with severe ADHD, I know it's a very real condition (and I used to believe it was a complete fad). Things like exercising, eating well (and regularly), sleeping well, and meditating can also help improve your overall concentration, health, and well-being. More about those in chapter 2, "Unlocking Health and Happiness." (Review that chapter if you want to improve your concentration!)

While on the topic of scheduling social media time—there's a time you should never be on social media. When?

When you are speaking with others.

There are few things as annoying as speaking to someone who won't look up from their phone.

If someone is having a conversation with you, honor them by looking at them and listening to what they have to say. Especially if they're trying to do something for you . . . like your dad trying to figure out when you need to be at soccer practice so that he can drive you and your friends there.

If, on the other hand, someone is trying to have a conversation with you when you're busy with something on your phone, then say so. "I'd love to speak with you, but please give me a few minutes to do this. Then we can talk."

Online Super Heroes, Fakes, and Reality

Social media is about the things we want to share. Naturally, we often want to share the good times. Shout from the rooftops about that great thing we just experienced.

That means that people don't always post about the boring stuff in their life. But everyone experiences it. Don't let yourself be fooled into thinking that people with great photos on social media live great lives. Plus, you can stink like a skunk and do a video where you look great on TikTok. You can take amazing photos of the food you cook while munching a very unhealthy chocolate bar. The person driving a Porsche on Insta might be sitting in the backseat five minutes after they stopped shooting the reel crying about their horrible mother who never cared, their father who is a drunk, or their brother who has severe mental health issues.

We all have difficult sides to our lives that we don't always show.

Don't think that people are perfect or lead perfect lives because their feed looks great. And certainly don't think you have to live your life like that. You do you. That's what you're best at.

What people put on social media isn't necessarily lies, but it's a selective truth. And possibly a few lies, too. Bear that in mind when scrolling.

So, get rid of the idea that others are perfect and you aren't.

Get rid of the idea that other people live perfect lives and you don't.

Get rid of the idea that everyone else is having a blast and you aren't.

Remember the stuff I said about actors? It's not the famous actors who are happy—it's the actors who enjoy acting who are happy. Don't mistake a big house or a fancy car for happiness! Doing what you love with the people you love is what makes you happy!

Also, remember what I said about empowering others through your posts? When people read or see your posts, they feel something. What do you want them to think and feel? You have the power to be a positive influence, so use it!

Social media shouldn't be about making yourself *look* great, but making others and yourself *feel* great.

Digital SOS

Some people, either to get attention or as a cry for help, will post about being depressed, suicidal, abused, or performing self-harm. It's like a digital SOS—a loud cry for help or a desperate plea for attention.

This isn't the same as sharing an experience—some people speak out about being depressed, but show their followers that they are getting help and are taking steps to get better. Those are people who want to open up so that others can get help and to challenge the stigma of mental health issues.

By the end of the day, mental health issues are simply brain chemicals that are unbalanced. This can happen because you were born with more or less of some chemicals, because of trauma, illness, or injury, or because of lifestyle choices. Changing your lifestyle, getting help from a psychologist, and, sometimes, taking doctor-prescribed medication can help balance the chemicals. It's important to take those steps, and people who are willing to go out there and share their experiences are rockstars for doing it!

That's very different from someone saying they're super sad and everything's horrible, they're going to kill themselves, or do self-harm. Those are the SOS posts. And sometimes people feel they have nowhere else to turn, so they turn to social media, which can be a good thing as it can alert people that they need

help. Because they do. Whether the person posting is seeking attention or actually feeling the way they say they do, they need professional help.

If you see a post like that, speak to an adult about it—you shouldn't have to deal with that kind of information alone. Ask the adult if they think you should raise the alarm to someone close to the person. Or if you know the person well, perhaps you can tell your parents you think it's time to do something, like speak with their parents, or the school.

Just bear in mind that you're not responsible for other people. If a person is depressed and does something bad, that's their choice. By the end of the day, they need to take responsibility for their life and get the help they need. Maybe they're incapable of doing that, but it's still not your responsibility.

Always offer a helping hand if you can, but don't put yourself in a position where you feel responsible for others. You're responsible for you. And if you have difficulty controlling your own anger, your sadness, your depression, or something else, seek out someone to talk to. If those close to you don't understand, or you don't wish to speak with them, speak to a counselor at school, call a hotline, or seek assistance from someone whom you hold in high regard. Remember that while you can vent to friends, they aren't professionally trained to help you. Seeking professional advice can make a world of difference. Teenage years can be filled with difficult emotions that can be made so much easier to handle if you have people supporting you through it.

Lastly, realize that even if people love you, they don't always have the answers. If you feel they can't help you, go elsewhere, but go to someone who is reputable. Don't ask someone who knows nothing about the topic, or can't keep their own life together, for advice.

When it comes to getting support online, instead of writing posts, look for information from verified professionals (such as psychologists and psychiatrists on Instagram, or therapists with blogs you can read) and for support groups to join. Facebook offers many different kinds of support groups. There are (often closed) support groups for people who grieve, people who are pregnant, families going through divorce, people with cancer, people whose parents have cancer, people with diabetes . . . The list goes on.

If you're unsure whether a group is for you, or if it offers content that is actually helpful, approach an adult who can advise you. Don't jump blindly into things. And remember—while everyone in a support group has a voice, not everyone will offer the best advice. For that, look for professionals and, even then, seek a second opinion from another professional if needed.

In short, if you need help with something, there are support groups online, but you should also talk to professionals offline if you can. Be open minded, but also question what you learn.

What you don't want to do is watch videos or read posts that reinforce the negative thoughts and feelings you have. For example, there are a ton of TikTok videos by depressed people talking about how depressed they are or how horrible life is. Content like that isn't going to help you, it will harm you.

When Content Turns Poisonous

If you follow people who post content that makes you feel like your life is horrible in comparison to theirs, it won't do you any good. No matter how nice and addictive the content is. Because every time you see their posts you think "OMG, my life stinks."

Likewise, if you follow people who you feel are better looking, stronger, or smarter than you, and use it as a measure against your own ugliness, weakness, or stupidity, then it isn't healthy. They aren't supposed to make you feel that way. Seeing people who give beauty tips, workout ideas, or show their smarts is supposed to *inspire* you!

When I was a teen, I read books and watched series, thinking some of the protagonists had really, really cool lives. But I didn't compare myself to them thinking I was inferior—instead, I got inspired and worked hard to become more like them.

Perhaps it's easier with fictional characters, because we know they aren't real. But it's actually the same with influencers and other people on social media—what they post is only *part of the truth.*

As I said earlier, most of us post what we're proud of, or simply want others to know. We build a persona online—showing ourselves off as we want others to see us. It's not *all* of who we are. And, if you think about it, there's always going to be someone who is prettier, fitter, smarter . . . That doesn't mean *you* aren't an incredible being. Your talents, when put together, amounts to something unique.

Another thing you have to remember when comparing yourself to others is that they don't have your family and friends. To your tribe, you're invaluable. They love you. Never mind if you're the smartest cookie in the cookie jar or the fittest person on the planet—they love you because of your personality traits and quirks.

Always, always remember this: To some people, your life and the ability to spend time with you is the most precious thing in the world. Even if you struggle to make friends right now, or have issues at home, one day, you'll find your tribe.

There's another form of toxic content that I briefly touched on earlier—content that makes us feel bad because it feeds negative thinking.

This could be watching lots of depressing videos or reading posts containing sad thoughts. It could be watching stuff that's about disasters if you fear them. It could be watching videos about people who have lost someone because you lost a family member. It could also be watching people obsess about losing weight and being thinner if you have an eating disorder, or don't have it yet, but might fall prey to it if you continue thinking the thoughts you do about your body.

Basically, it's any content that feeds your own sadness, fear, depression, or other negative habits in your life. While it can be good to find people who have been through something similar that you have, it's not good to be sucked into content that confirms that life is sad or is all about losing weight, or whatever it might be. You want to find people who have had similar experiences *and* are better now.

Hard times can actually help us become happier if we learn from them.

If you think you have a difficult relationship with food, watch videos that encourage a healthy relationship to food and videos from people who have overcome eating disorders, unless even that triggers you. A psychologist will be able to help you find what works for you.

If you feel down, blue, or depressed, watch videos from people who have overcome mood disorders and depression. Better yet—seek help. Some people feel down because they have SAD (seasonal affective disorder). Basically, in winter they don't feel well. Others feel down because they've experienced trauma.

What I'm trying to say is that there are many different reasons for feeling depressed. Unless you know the cause, it can be hard to fix it. There are things that can make us all feel better (as mentioned in chapter 2), but certain things need specific treatment. For example, people who have SAD need special lamps that mimic sunlight to help them feel good in winter.

Another form of negative content is the kind of content you feel you have to watch all the time. This could be fashion content in case you're a fashion influencer—you think if you miss a single post, you're out of the loop. It could be your friends' updates—unless you stay on top, you are excluded. It can be any kind of content where you feel you either have to stay up to date or engage in the conversation or you'll be excluded or miss out.

That brings us to the next part: FoMO—fear of missing out. Some people feel that if they take a break from social media, even for a moment, they will miss something.

It's not necessarily that the content is toxic, *the toxic part is the need to stay on top of every feed at all hours.*

The ironic thing?

> If you're always on social media, you're missing out on what's in front of you. It's just that you've started thinking your life is all about social media, so you feel your life is online.

Having FoMO can lead to anxiety, disrupted sleep, and lots of other things that negatively impact your mental health.

In short, FoMO can make you feel bad and lose out on real life relationships as you ignore them in favor of being online. Maybe you even give up on activities you love and hobbies because you feel you need to be online instead.

If you feel that social media is taking over your life and you're unable to be fully present in the moment, it's time to do something about it.

As a first line of action, try to schedule social media time, like I mentioned earlier. Basically, set the times you are allowed online every day, such as for five minutes once an hour and one hour at night.

Also, do some meditation and try the other tips mentioned in chapter 2. Mindfulness exercises as well as physical exercise help us feel good. That, in turn, means we don't need the "kick" we get from social media as much.

It might sound strange—why would meditating and exercising help me stay off social media? Obsessive behaviors usually mean some brain chemistry is out of whack. Doing things that replenish our "happy chemicals" can therefore make us feel like we don't "need" to do the thing we previously thought we had to do.

Another tip is to sign up for some new hobby where you can't use a phone (a bit tricky when playing soccer, wrestling, dancing, or riding a horse, for example)—that can also take your mind off social media by engaging it in something else.

Yet another strategy is to try a "social media detox" together with a friend or family member. Decide together how much social media you're allowed, if any. You could choose to delete the social media app for a while so you can focus on your detox. You could even have your parents take your phones and tablets away and only give them to you for certain periods of time.

Research shows that to create new habits, it's best if you make it *easy* (i.e. don't sit by yourself in your bedroom doing nothing while staring at your phone—then staying off social media is hard), do it together with others, and reward yourself every so often if you get it right.

Find that doesn't work? You just can't stop thinking about social media and panic at the thought of missing out on online stuff? Get professional help.

Social media can turn into an addiction and as with any addiction, it's easier to stop it early on. There are a ton of techniques that can help you overcome addiction, and professionals can help you apply them.

What's more, if you're hyper-focused on social media, there might be an underlying reason. Perhaps, you're really stressed or sad about something else in your life and social media is your coping mechanism. Meaning you spend time online so that you don't have to think about the part of your life that's bugging you.

Basically, social media is a way to distract yourself. Sometimes distraction is good (it's better to watch a comedy than get stuck in a thought loop about how awful you are at something), but it should only be used as a temporary thing. You have to deal with the underlying thought (you're not awful). Meaning you have to face the stuff that's making you feel upset. But not get stuck mulling it over forever—just face it and move on. But in a healthy way, doing things that truly make you feel good, not just things that distract you from the bad stuff.

Social media can be a wonderful tool; it's just important to ensure it's used correctly. Stay safe and use it to connect with friends and family, learn from and connect with people outside your social circle, and build your network. Avoid risky behaviors and posting things you'll later regret. And be sure that social media is a *part* of your life, not all your life—schedule time for having fun online *and* offline.

PART 4
PRACTICAL LIVING

8

Turning Chores into Tasks You Actually (Almost) Want to Do

Tips on how to handle household chores and cleaning

We've gotten to the part of the book that might make your eyes glaze over as you stare into space considering what to message your friend, how to build a kite, what to wear to a party, or even that one math equation that is more interesting than cleaning the house.

But . . . here's the deal (I say that a lot, don't I?): if you become effective at doing things you don't enjoy, you do them faster. So, let's help you become effective.

Tackling What You Don't Like Doing

Here are some tips for doing chores when you don't want to . . . and how to do them faster while having more fun!

1. Do them *before* you do the fun stuff.
2. Break them down into easily achievable chunks (clean the kitchen on a Monday, the living room on a Tuesday, and so forth).
3. Deal with things right away, instead of letting things build up (see above—it's easier to spend five minutes a day doing the dishes, than an hour on a Sunday night when you'd like to chill).

4. Get organized—write down what day and time you do what.

5. Put yourself in a happy frame of mind—be on a call with a friend, listen to an audiobook, or listen to some music while you cook, clean, take out the rubbish, or sort your receipts. BUT every so often, do your chores with no distraction and see if it doesn't work as a sort of meditation (yeah, seriously—hard work can be meditative).

6. Time yourself—the key to not cleaning at sloth pace is to set a timer. Challenge yourself to see how fast you can get stuff done. It's also clever to schedule it before doing something you love, like meeting a friend, as it will put you in a good mood and make you more energetic as you hurry so you can get to the fun stuff.

7. Reward yourself every so often when you've completed a task you dislike.

8. Get someone to hold you accountable.

Creating Cool Checklists for Everyday Chores

Checklists aren't cool, are they?

Actually, they kinda are.

A study found that having checklists at the ER/surgery could help lower the mortality rate.

That's pretty cool, isn't it? (It's also pretty terrifying that the mortality goes up when they don't have checklists!)

And did you know that plenty of parents forget their kids in their car? Our brains run on autopilot, so if we don't have a system we always follow (and most people don't *always* have their kid in the car), we easily forget things. Such as a sleeping child. (Which is why it's recommended to leave your purse, phone, and keys next to the child, as you'll usually need at least one of those the moment you step out of the car.)

Of course you're thinking this will never happen to you, right? Only, it will. If your routine is not set in stone and the absolute same every day, you will forget things. Even important things. Which is why doctors end up making mistakes that cost lives and parents leave their kids in the car by accident.

The cool thing is that checklists can help you with just about anything.

If you find that every morning you seem to remember that you didn't pack something for school the night before, have a checklist for your bag. If there are gym bags and other stuff you need to bring on certain days, make a checklist for each day of the week.

If you're prone to leaving the lights, stove, or anything else on, have a checklist by the door and make it a *habit* to check it before you leave. Seriously. Not just a reminder (because you'll forget to look at it after a while), but a checklist that you have to *tick off.*

If you have chores you need to perform around the house (which you will have the moment you leave home, if not sooner), make a checklist for those. When do you need to clean the fridge and check you haven't got something growing mold in there? When is it time to flush the drains? When do you need to wash the windows? When do you need to buy yourself a treat to celebrate getting things done that week?

You can have daily, weekly, and monthly checklists. Just use your diary or calendar app.

You can also put up a big wall calendar where you mark important things so that it's easy to see. Another tip is to set reminders on your phone. Wall calendars are great as you can see them and get a feel for what's happening when (a totality—with weekly calendars, we tend to look only at what's happening right now). Phones are great as they offer reminders before a certain event takes place and remind us to show up or prepare.

Checklists don't only help us remember what needs to get done and ensure it does indeed get done, they also help us do things faster, as does proper planning—marking out what to do when in our calendars. When we don't have to figure out what to do next or in what order we should do things, we become a lot faster at what we're doing. That's why time-saving enthusiasts plan their wardrobe a week in advance—that way, there's no time wasted when deliberating what to wear in the morning!

You'll be surprised by how much more effective you will become and how much more time you'll have if you get organized with checklists.

EXERCISE

Make a checklist for at least one area of your life. You might also want to have a sneak peek at time management in chapter 13 and combine the two exercises.

Tips for Tidying Up

One of the best tips you'll ever get for tidying is to put things away *right away* so you don't have to run around tidying things up later!

To keep things tidy, have a space for each item. If you don't want to sort items, such as your socks, have a basket or a box where you can toss them all in. It's much easier to keep things tidy if you're organized. What's more, if you don't know where to put things and therefore where to find them, you'll spend hours looking for them.

If you want to make your life simple, cut the clutter. Every single item you own needs dusting unless it's in a glass cabinet or cupboard. Enough said.

If you want a tidy wardrobe, pack away the winter clothes when summer arrives and vice versa.

Cleaning

As mentioned in the beginning of this chapter, if you dislike cleaning, you might not want to do *all* the cleaning in a day. You can do one task a day, if you prefer. It depends on how you feel about it—some people prefer doing it all in one go, some people prefer spending ten minutes a day on it.

When it comes to detergents, you can often make your own—you just google what you need (floor cleaner, window cleaner, etc.) and you'll find recipes online. I've also mentioned some tips for homemade detergents below. However, always check the surface before you start scrubbing away with homemade detergents. Vinegar and water make for a great detergent, but certain types of wood and stone don't like vinegar as it's an acid (meaning the vinegar might destroy the surface).

The reason for making your own detergents? Saving money, the environment, and possibly your health. Basically, they aren't as toxic as many of the detergents you buy.

Thankfully, there are a lot of non-toxic products on the market today, as well. Just read the labels—the non-toxic ones are normally labeled as eco-friendly or natural, but it's not always the case that products with those labels are non-toxic, so really do make sure to read the label and do some research surrounding what can be called toxic. Remember that sometimes ingredients that are toxic in large amounts can be useful in small amounts, such as having bleach handy when someone gets sick as you need to disinfect a room.

Also, remember that certain essential oils used in natural products might not be good for your pets and can cause allergies in humans, too. Again, read the label and do your research. For example, tea tree oil has antibacterial and antifungal properties and is good for many things ranging from Athlete's foot to cleaning, it truly has a lot of uses, but it can be deadly for pets, shouldn't be used around children, and can cause allergies.

The two main things you need to do around the house (beyond washing and doing your dishes) are dusting and cleaning the floors. So let's look at tips for those.

Tips for dusting:

- Dust before you clean the floors as any dust that gets stirred up and falls on the floors will then be cleaned up.
- Using a feather duster will send dust into the air, and when it lands again . . . your home will be as dusty as it was before you dusted.
- Special dry cloths for dusting are available in shops, or simply use a moist towel—something that doesn't scratch the furniture.
- Water will clean away dust—you don't need harsh chemicals.

- If you want to get rid of some fungi or bacteria, water mixed with tea tree oil and vinegar (and other essential oils if you like) is a good option, just be sure you read up about whatever essential oils you use (as mentioned earlier, pets and tea tree oil do not go together).
- If you have furniture made with stone, such as marble and granite, don't use vinegar as it can dull the stone over time. The same goes for wooden furniture.
- If you need to get rid of some grease (not dust), baking soda and water or dishwashing liquid and water should do the trick. Just wipe it off with water when done.

Tips for cleaning the floors:

- Start with vacuuming or sweeping.
- Then mop or wipe the floors, but don't use so much water you soak them! You don't need a detergent if the floors aren't all that dirty.
- Every so often, use the correct detergent (whether homemade or store bought) for your particular floors—linoleum, wooden floors, terracotta tiles, etc. all need different detergents.
- If you have rugs, vacuuming them is the way to go. Depending on the rug, you might also want to wash it or steam it from time to time (look up how to care for your rug). On the odd chance you don't have a vacuum cleaner, you'll need to hang your rugs up outside and give it some good whacks to get the dust out. Even if you have a vacuum cleaner, you might want to do that from time to time. And be sure to clean or change your vacuum filter regularly.
- If you have carpeted floors, vacuuming them regularly and steaming them once a year should suffice.

How often should you clean the floors? That depends on how much dust and dirt floats about in your home—some places get dustier so much faster. And if you have a pet that sheds hair or if you share your home with a lot of people, it gets dirtier faster. Vacuuming or sweeping the floors at least once a week and mopping them at least once every other week is a good starting point.

That said, if you see your floors getting dirty daily because lots of people use the same space, then that's how often they need to be cleaned.

A tip to keep your home clean is to remove your shoes when you come inside. Another tip is to clean the kitchen floor more often if you're prone to spilling things (and stuff like flour have a way of floating about even if you don't spill them) that then get dragged around the house.

When it comes to the bathroom, it is slightly unique because it can get invaded by mold and bacteria. Here, good sanitizers and mold busters come in handy for the toilet, bathtub, sink, and shower. You can use natural mixtures such as water mixed with vinegar, tea tree oil, baking soda, and castile soap. You can also use something harsher, like bleach, or a detergent especially for the bathroom.

Make sure your bathroom is ventilated. If you don't have a powerful ventilator, open the window. Otherwise, as it's moist in there, chances are mold will develop.

Needless to say, if someone is having a stomach bug, get some bleach and clean the toilet after each use!

Then there's the kitchen. You dust it and clean the floors like every other place in the house, but you need to wipe down surfaces you use (such as the kitchen counter, cooker, or table) after each use. Basically, whenever you make a mess or spill some food, wipe it up.

As for the fridge, that probably needs a good clean once a month or so. The oven will also need a wipe down once a month or once every other month. You need to buy an oven cleaner for that, unless you have a self-cleaning oven. They are harsh and not nice to use, but they do get rid of anything stuck to the inside of the oven (and the top of the stove).

There's usually a lot of oily and fatty spills in the kitchen, but thankfully, plain old dishwashing liquid can take care of most of those.

How do you clean windows? Mix two parts of water with one part of white vinegar in a spray bottle, spray your window, and wipe down with a soft cloth (such as a microfiber cloth) till dry. Alternatively, use warm (not hot) water and mix in a little bit of dishwashing liquid (with emphasis on little), and then dry. If you have any greasy spots, you can simply use dishwashing liquid just there and then rinse off with water.

Speaking of windows—always air out your home. For you to have healthy air in your home (unless you live in a very polluted area), the best thing to do is to open your windows. Yes, even if you have an aircon. Why? Because air conditioners have filters. Filters that get dirty. So do replace them often. But even if you do, nothing beats fresh air.

Another way to clean the air in your home is to buy plants that are specifically good at this, such as chrysanthemums (careful though as they are toxic to animals), spider plants, and golden pothos. How effective they are at cleaning the air is debated, but they do some good.

Lastly, the insides of cupboards and other spots you might not wipe down frequently should be cleaned at least every six months or so (kitchen cupboards might get dirty sooner and the chest of drawers you rarely use might not need to be cleaned that often). Do the traditional spring clean and Christmas clean. Some clean when there's an equinox in spring and winter, some before certain holidays, others simply set a date (it helps to invite lots of friends to help you out and end with a pizza party to celebrate the effort).

Laundry

The main thing to remember when doing the laundry?

Read the instructions.

Different clothes need different types of washing—it will say on the label what they need. Your washing machine will then tell you what kind of washes it offers in the instruction manual (so yes, you might actually have to read that thing instead of throwing it away . . . but don't worry if you already did so, most manuals can be found online these days).

Some clothes can't be washed; they need to be taken to a dry cleaners. The label will tell you what to do.

Some clothes can be tumble dried, some can't. Again, read the label.

There are some more basic things to remember:

1. The higher the temperature, the more likely something will shrink.
2. The higher the speed of spinning something, the more likely something will get ruined.
3. You can use bleach to freshen up whites, but nothing else.
4. If you spill something, immediately look up how to remove it as different types of spots need to be handled differently (you can buy some spot removers or use whatever is recommended).
5. If something is heavily soiled, you might need a spot remover before you wash it.
6. The first few times you wash something really colorful (such as a bright pink top), you might want to wash it with other clothes that have a similar color as it might "bleed" color during the wash and discolor other items.
7. Always wash dark clothes with other dark clothes, and light clothes with other light clothes.
8. Dryer sheets can be bad for people with sensitive skin, the dryer itself, and the envirement. Look into using wool dryer balls instead. Oh, and remember to always clean the lint trap and hose (many home fires start this way).

Oh, and just for the record—laundry doesn't do itself. Unfortunately. You're going to have to simply get used to doing it. Or take it to the laundrette.

Keeping an Eye on Maintenance and Handling Emergencies

Blocked toilet on a Saturday night.

Leaking pipe on a Friday night.

Suddenly no power on a Sunday morning.

Those are all things you might have to deal with when you have a home of your own. And you often have to make the decision of whether to fix something yourself or call someone in to fix it (though if you're renting, you can often call the landlord or estate agency instead).

If you aren't a plumber, electrician, or roof repair person, trying to do DIY can go two ways.

In the best possible scenario, you fix the problem while saving money doing it yourself.

In the worst-case scenario, you end up spending hours figuring out what to do and buying materials, only to botch the job.

Of course, you can also land somewhere in between—a half decent job that saves you some money.

If you're unsure whether you should do it yourself (and it can pay off in the long run to learn some things), ask people who know. Also, use Google to do some research. What are other people saying about doing this kind of thing themselves? And note that some handymen say you can't do it because they want you to hire them to do it, but if "regular" people are also saying it's difficult or authoritative websites say it's downright dangerous, then don't attempt it.

Maintenance, on the other hand, you need to learn about (or hire someone to have a look at your house regularly). I'm not saying you should learn how to do all the maintenance yourself, but you need to know what needs doing when and have a budget in place for it.

If you're getting your first place to rent, or even buy, ask someone who knows what they are talking about, what to look out for, and what needs maintenance when. Each home is different and needs different care.

Perhaps your electrical wiring should be looked into in the next six months.

Perhaps your windowsills need sanding and painting soon.

Perhaps the plumbing requires some maintenance. For example, I have this thing outside where some of my pipes converge (I don't even know what you'd call it, it's a drain of sorts). It needs cleaning every so often. In other places where I've lived, I haven't had something like that.

When it comes to plumbing, people say that some vinegar mixed with baking soda and boiling hot water works wonders for maintenance and to remove small blockages. Personally, I've never found it to remove blockages, while drain uncloggers bought in the store have worked wonders. They also damage some drains, especially if used often. So if you have a landlord/lady, you might want to check with them first if you can use them.

If you want to try the vinegar and baking soda approach, simply pour one pot of boiling hot water down the drain, followed by one cup of baking soda and one cup of vinegar. Cover the drain with the plug. Wait five minutes. Unplug the plug. Pour another pot of hot water down the drain.

If there's a blocked drain, my first call of action is to use a plunger to see if there's a blockage near the sink or tub that will come loose with the help of one. This is also a good approach for a blocked toilet (and yes, go get a plunger—you should have one at home at all times).

My second go-to is the abovementioned drain unclogger. After using one (you usually have to leave them overnight), I tend to mix dishwashing liquid with hot water to flush it out. Why? Because if there's soap or fat coating the insides of the drain, that can help get rid of it. That's also a good maintenance technique, as is the abovementioned vinegar and baking soda approach (while it might not remove major drain blockages, it can help clean your drains and pipes and *prevent* blockages).

You can clean your drains once a week with boiling water (people recommend pouring half a pot, waiting five minutes, then pouring another—add dishwashing liquid if you like) and use the vinegar and baking soda method once a month. You can also buy a detergent for that purpose.

While speaking of maintenance, some vinegar and hot water can get rid of calcium buildup in your kettle (yes, even a kettle needs maintenance!).

Each home is different. Figure out the main things in your home that you need to keep an eye on, and when emergencies happen (and they do, so budget for them), make an educated decision whether you want to deal with them yourself or bring in a professional.

NOTE

Certain things are dangerous. Fixing a leak on the roof requires you to be in a harness to prevent you from falling if you slip. If you fix electrical wiring and it goes wrong, you can set the house on fire (and not necessarily while you're fixing it but days or months later, so you might not be at home or you might be asleep when it happens) or electrocute yourself—and even die. If the plumbing goes wrong, you can end up with a flooded home. So evaluate the risks and learn what precautions are needed before you do something yourself.

9

Kitchen Manners: Basic Kitchen Know-How

Some thoughts around food and how to cook and handle it

If the thought of cooking makes you want to run screaming out the door, don't worry. It's not as hard as it seems. But before you even get started on cooking, you need to learn the basics of food handling and kitchen safety. Don't worry—it's not rocket science. It's just common sense, really, but if you haven't spent a lot of time in the kitchen, you might not know it.

Below is some food for thought (no pun intended). Once you've digested this, you can start getting creative in the kitchen!

Don't Burn the Food . . . or the House

Let's start with the essentials—staying safe when cooking.

First, get a smoke alarm . . . or several. You should really have one in every room of your home (and batteries should be changed every six months). You should have fire extinguishers in at least two rooms of the house, too (more if your house is large). A fire blanket can also be good in the kitchen, as you can throw it over something that's caught fire.

If you use gas in your home, get an alarm for that, too. Place it near where gas could leak, such as in the kitchen if you have a gas stove.

To ensure you don't burn anything while cooking, get an egg timer or a phone with a timer on it. Always time your cooking. As someone who has burnt water, I am a big fan of this (and of whistling kettles, so you don't leave while waiting for the water to boil and forget that you were making a cup of tea in the first place). It's so easy to pick up your phone and start scrolling on Facebook while you wait for your cake to get done, only to look up ten minutes later when you smell something burning. Always set a timer!

Another classic mistake is removing a pot and leaving the stove on. You might want to invest in a stove that automatically turns itself off . . . but failing that, make a point of always double checking that the stove is off once you're done cooking. Once it becomes a habit, you tend to do it automatically.

Last, but not least, always check that the stove is off before going to bed or leaving the house. It might sound silly, but a lot of fires could have been prevented that way. Just as we think we'd never leave our kid in the car, we think we'd never leave the stove on, but it happens all the time. You get a phone call that distracts you. You start responding to a message, and before stopping to think, you've walked away from the kitchen without checking if anything is still on.

It comes back to the checklists I mentioned in another chapter—by having a checklist to tick off, we can't forget (unless we forget to check the checklist). So pop a checklist by your bed or by the door and ensure you tick it off.

The Basics of Cooking Oils and Some Cooking Techniques

As for the health aspects, various oils have different pros and cons, but what everyone agrees upon is that hydrogenated oils are considered unhealthy (but can be great in cosmetics, on the other hand) and olive oil seems to be considered "good for you." Of course, it's still an oil, so it's good for you when used in moderation!

Apart from having different flavor profiles (and truly, the only way to get to know those is to use different oils to find out what they taste like and, of course, follow recipes that suggest one oil over another), what you need to know about oils is that they have different smoking points. Basically, when an oil hits a certain temperature, it starts to smoke. That's also when it breaks down and starts releasing free radicals (those aren't good for your body, but antioxidants found in some plants, fruits, and vegetables tend to counteract them).

In other words, you don't want to heat an oil to the point when it starts smoking. That's why it's important to choose the right oil for the heat you'll be using when cooking.

Some oils with really high smoking points are:

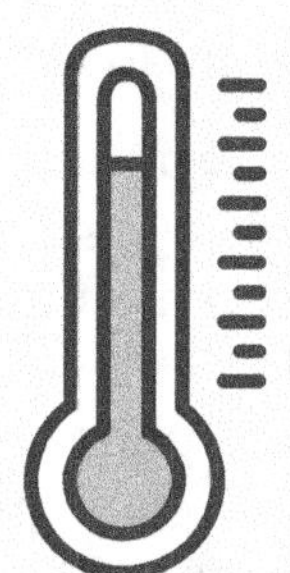

- Refined avocado oil (480–520°F or 248–271°C)
- Refined safflower oil (450–500°F or 232–260°C)
- Refined and semi-refined sunflower oil (450°F or 232°C)
- Clarified butter (450°F or 232°C)
- Refined peanut oil (450°F or 232°C)
- Refined sesame oil (410°F or 210°C)
- Soy oil (450°F or 232°C)

On the low side (i.e. a low smoking point), you have unrefined and raw oils, such as extra virgin, cold-pressed, or unrefined coconut, olive, safflower, peanut, sesame, canola or rapeseed, corn, and sunflower oil. Butter and lard also fall in this category. Of these, olive oil, lard, corn oil, and coconut oil have the highest smoke points.

How do you best prepare your food? Should you boil it, fry it, sear it, bake it, steam it, or even eat it raw?

That depends on the dish you're making. Different cooking methods bring out different flavors in the food. Look at a couple of recipes and then make a decision.

What's more, cooking food alters its nutrient profile.

Eating a lot of raw fruit and vegetables is likely good for you (especially as the enzymes found in the foods are still intact), but cooked foods are easier to digest. And some cooked foods are great as the cooking helps bring out certain nutrients (especially ones that are soluble in water or fat). Basically, the nutrient profile changes as things are cooked because nutrients dissolve into the water or oil.

I could write an entire chapter on what vitamins and minerals are lost when the food is heated and which become more accessible. Instead of overwhelming you, just bear in mind that if you approach it in a balanced way—eat raw salads and fruits but also enjoy cooked meals full of vegetables and some fruits—chances are you'll do well. You can also google it if you want to find out more information.

If you want to keep as many nutrients as possible when cooking something, steaming, baking, or stir-frying (frying it for a minute or so on very high heat) is recommended. Boiling tends to release nutrients into the water (so unless it's a soup or stew, they're lost), and frying adds too much fat.

Understanding How to Pick Fresh Ingredients

Why do chefs buy their food at markets instead of the supermarket? Because they're fresher and there's a better selection so they can always pick the best ingredients.

Now, I'm no chef, so I can't tell you what the perfectly ripe strawberry should look and smell like, but I can give you some general pointers.

Not so fresh or too fresh (unripe):

- Green potatoes (poisonous)
- Green bananas (unripe)
- Wilted greens (unfresh)
- Vegetables and fruits that develop brown spots (either they've been bruised or they're getting old . . . but certain fruits like some persimmons are the exception to the rule . . . and some fruits with brown spots, such as bananas, pears, and apples, can be used for cooking)
- Green stuff growing on the products (mold—and if a bread is green in one end, it's got "invisible" mold throughout and not just where it's green)
- It smells wrong (milk, for example, stinks if it gets too old)
- Clear liquids turn cloudy (like milk or cream—you can see it if you pour it into coffee as it will look like there are dots or clouds in there)

There's also a difference between fresh, raw, pasteurized, irradiated, and so forth.

You will find that there are oils that are refined and unrefined. Refined means some chemical process has been used to treat it. Unrefined (such as extra virgin olive oil) means that the oil has not been processed—whatever came out when the olives were pressed is what you'll find in the bottle. Cold-pressed means no heat was used in the process.

Some labels say the food is raw. That usually means it hasn't been heated or treated. For example, some honey is pasteurized to ensure it doesn't crystalize so easily, while milk is pasteurized because it kills off bacteria. In fact, many people choose to buy raw honey because it has not been heated and, therefore, should there be health benefits to raw honey, they get them while eating it.

Some honey, as well as spices, have been irradiated. That means ionized radiation has been applied to the product to kill off any insects, fungi, or bacteria and to increase its shelf life. Some people claim it also removes some of the health benefits. You will find that some supermarkets proudly label their spices as non-irradiated.

To find out if something is raw or has been treated, you need to read the label.

The Importance of Reading Food Labels

Labels are super important. Why? Because if you don't read them, you have no idea what goes into the food you're eating. And what goes into the food you buy at the supermarket can sometimes be shocking.

Below you'll find a list to help you "decode" labels. Just remember that labels are different everywhere. You have to check what is required to get something labeled organic where you live, for example.

- Grass-fed—the animals have been fed grass, not grains or other foods (in some cases some grains may be allowed).
- Free range—the animals have been allowed a certain amount of time outdoors or live in an open barn (as opposed to

being in a cage or standing still in a stable). Note that the restrictions vary in different countries and how much time spent outdoors and the amount of space required varies (in some countries, very little outdoor time and space is required for this label, so basically the animals are free to move about but they're packed as sardines . . . well, perhaps not that bad, but you get the idea).

- Organic—when it comes to plants, only special pesticides are allowed, such as non-harmful ones that are made from mostly organic compounds, while when it comes to meat, the animals are only fed foods labeled organic or wild, no hormones or antibiotics are allowed, and they need to be raised in living conditions that allow them to partake in natural behaviors (if it's something like a deodorant that's labeled organic, most of the ingredients in it need to be organic).

- Fairtrade—indicates certain rules have been followed with regards to pricing and fair treatment of workers, as well as certain environmental standards.

- Wild—it has been foraged or hunted in nature as opposed to having been grown or raised on a farm.

- Hormones—hormones, such as growth hormones, have been added to the feed of the animals.

- Antibiotics—antibiotics have been fed to the animals to cure or prevent illness.

- Halal—the food has been prepared according to certain Muslim principles.

- Kosher—the food has been prepared according to certain Jewish standards.

- All natural—this is a bit tricky because there are no regulations for this label in most places. Usually, it indicates that the product contains natural products, not man-made chemicals, additives, etc. Some additives are natural as they occur naturally in nature but not necessarily good for you or it has a natural source but is super refined (like xylitol which is natural but super refined).

- Fragrance or perfume—indicates that the product contains chemically made scents.

- Naturally scented or natural perfume—indicates that the product contains natural substances that give it its fragrance, such as essential oils, or ground dried flowers.

- Food grade—usually indicates it's safe to eat or, when it comes to products such as spatulas, that they can be used with food (i.e. come in contact with food without contaminating it), but some essential oils have been labeled food grade even if the effects of consuming them have not been proven—they are just generally considered safe when used as directed.

Note that companies might label something organic but what they refer to is that an organic compound has been used, not that the product is made with organic ingredients. For example, you can use organic fibers (found in plants) to make fabric, but then you can dye it using chemicals. And the plants themselves might not have been grown *organically.*

Companies often try marketing ploys, especially with claims like "natural" that they aren't likely to get sued for using, even if the product isn't strictly natural.

Also note that just because something is natural, or organic, doesn't mean it's better, or even good, for you. Certain essential oils have been proven to have helpful *and/or* harmful effects on people. Most essential oils in moderation are good for you, but too much can cause problems. And some people are allergic to various essential oils. Plus, some essential oils can kill certain pets and should never come in contact with babies.

This is why it's so important to do your research on *how* to use something.

Understanding Food Safety

Alright, so chances are raw eggs, milk, or meat are *not* going to suddenly explode or freak you out in the night, but they certainly can give you a scare and a very upset tummy if you eat them when they've gone off, haven't been cooked properly, or were contaminated. In fact, they could end up killing you if it's bad enough. I'm not trying to scare you—usually, the worst that will happen is an upset tummy—but there are cases of food poisoning that have been fatal. That's why it's important to know how to handle food properly.

First, let's look at what can or cannot be eaten raw:

- Sushi and sashimi are traditionally made with the types of fish (and in some instances, shellfish) that can be eaten raw, but if you make it yourself, it should be made with sushi-grade or sashimi-grade fish that has been *frozen* first. (Note that there is plenty of seafood that CANNOT be eaten raw.)
- Raw meat—red meat like duck, ostrich, and beef can be eaten raw, but special care should be taken and you should know that the meat comes from a reputable farm or shop and you need to ensure it's fresh when you eat it (especially with the birds, as they can contain salmonella).
- Eggs can be eaten raw, but again, you need to be careful as they can contain salmonella (wash and dry the eggs before you crack them, as salmonella is often on the outside of the shell).
- White meat, like chicken and pork, *cannot* be eaten raw.
- Milk can be drunk raw, but it can contain foodborne illnesses that, worst-case scenario, can kill you. So if you choose to drink it raw, choose a good dairy product from a reputable farm.
- Cheese can definitely be eaten raw. (Note that you can get sick from raw cheese, but it's unlikely, and it's not as dangerous as raw milk.)

When you are pregnant or breastfeeding, you should not eat these things raw. Small children should also avoid these kinds of raw foods.

If you choose to eat something raw, it needs to be fresh. No old meat. No old eggs. No old dairy. Fish is the exception as freezing it can kill off some parasites, but it needs to be frozen when it's fresh and you can't keep it in the freezer for too long.

On the topic of what can be eaten raw, certain restaurants will ask you if you want the meat rare, medium, or well-done. A rare steak is raw on the inside. A medium one still oozes blood but has been cooked for some time. A well done one is cooked through and through.

Some meats are considered best eaten rare or medium. Should you wish to eat rare or medium cooked meats, choose reputable suppliers or restaurants.

Some fish, such as tuna and salmon, are often served seared, which means they're only lightly fried (they're raw in the middle). The fish should have been frozen first. Why only sear it? It's juicier that way. Tuna becomes incredibly hard if you fry it till it's well done.

Veggies can obviously be eaten raw in most cases (there are some, like white potatoes, that need to be cooked), but they should always be washed in fresh, clean water first. Honestly, even if something says it's been washed, it's always best to give it a rinse yourself if you can. There was a scandal in one country recently where they found that the "washed" salad wasn't very clean at all.

Another important aspect of food safety is handling the food correctly and taking precautions when cooking it to prevent yourself from getting burned or injured. Below are some simple guidelines:

- Always wash your hands with soap and warm water before handling food, or use a hand sanitizer that you rinse off with water as you don't want it ending up in your food (and if you touch stuff in between when handling food, wash your hands again).
- Always wash anything that comes in contact with raw meat and eggs, including your hands.
- Remove rings and anything else that might touch the food before handling it.
- Take a step back when frying—you don't want oil splattered across you and especially not in your eyes.
- If using a blender, never ever stick something into the blender when you turn it on (like a spoon, or worse—your fingers), and always put the lid on properly or it will splatter the entire kitchen.

- Only use microwave-safe items in a microwave (if it's plastic, it usually has a symbol showing if it's microwave safe) and never use metal unless it's specified as microwave safe.
- Use an oven mitt when touching something hot, like a pan.
- Don't leave things with plastic parts leaning against a hot pan as it will melt (such as a spatula with a plastic handle when frying).
- Let food cool to room temperature before putting it in the fridge. Hot food cools down too slowly, which can lead to foodborne illnesses.
- Cover things you put in the fridge (such as using a container with a lid).
- Look up how long something will last in the fridge or freezer before eating it.
- Don't lick a spoon and then put it into food others will eat or food you are going to keep (such as a jar of marmalade or peanut butter) to avoid food contamination or bacterial growth.

Is It Done Yet? How to Check If the Food Is Ready

How do you know if something is cooked?

As a general rule, you want vegetables to be crunchy. Meaning they aren't soft or falling apart nor are they hard. How long that will take for different vegetables and cooking styles can easily be checked online.

Potatoes are done when you can stick a knife through them without feeling any resistance in the middle (i.e. they don't have a hard center anymore).

Breads and cakes are usually done when you can "stick a stick" in them and it comes out clean. That said, some cakes, such as mud cake, should be runny in the middle. You need to check the recipe. Many breads and cakes should also start to brown (get a crust).

Eggs . . . are a science. Everyone likes theirs differently. As eggs can be eaten raw, some like them runny. Others like them well-cooked—whether fried or boiled. When you fry, you will see how the consistency changes. If you're boiling an egg, this is a general guide:

- 3 minutes for a really soft boiled egg yolk and almost set egg white
- 4 minutes for a runny egg yolk and lightly set egg white
- 5 minutes for a gooey egg yolk and firm egg white
- 6 minutes for a softly set egg yolk and hard boiled egg white
- 7 minutes for a hard boiled egg

Meat, if well done, is ready if you see that the outside and inside have the same color when cooked. That might not be the best wording, especially as the outside might start to brown, so let's look at an example. If you fry a piece of chicken, you'll see that as soon as it touches the frying pan, it goes from pink to white. The inside of the chicken also needs to turn white, and there should be no blood when you cut it. All white meats should be well done.

When it comes to red meat that you want to serve rare or medium rare, you can look up the optimal time needed for that particular meat and thickness of meat.

Certain meats (whether rare, medium rare, or well done) are best checked by using a thermometer that you insert into the middle of the piece of meat you're cooking. You can buy a thermometer at your local supermarket or at more specialized cookware stores. You have to google the specific temperature of the meat you're looking to cook.

White fish tends to go from being almost translucent to white when you cook it. It should be white through and through. As different fish have different colors, check the outside of what you're cooking—the inside should turn the same color when done (and the outside might start to brown at that point).

> **TIPS** No matter what you cook, set a timer. It's only too easy to do something else and forget you have something on the stove.

Hopefully, this chapter has given you a taste (no pun intended) of a few things you need to learn when cooking. An important thing to remember, however, is to always look things up. If you're cooking pork for the first time, look up a couple of different recipes, as well as tips for cooking pork, before you settle on what to cook and how to cook it. If you don't know how long a cooked chicken will last in the fridge, look it up. If you're going to go buy bananas and want to find out what a perfectly ripe banana looks like, look it up.

It's also worth investing in a simple cookbook or finding a few recipes on Pinterest or on cooking blogs that you want to try out. You can also ask friends and relatives for their favorite recipes (it can be fun to collect those in a scrapbook). Remember to start with recipes that require few ingredients and don't take three hours to cook.

Then, slowly, build up the repertoire of dishes you can cook like a pro. As with everything else, you don't have to master everything in one go. Learn one new recipe a week or a month. Take it at your own pace.

Want to learn some of the basics of Western cooking? Check YouTube videos of Julia Child. If nothing else, you'll have a good giggle seeing the outdated videos. She's the woman "who taught America how to cook." In the book and film *Julie and Julia*, you can learn about her private life and, possibly, find some inspiration.

In general, YouTube is great for looking up how to cook just about anything.

Of course, if you want to try some of the recipes from the Blue Zones that are mentioned in the chapter "Unlocking Health and Happiness," you can go to their website.

Learn one recipe at a time and you'll do great!

Navigating the World of Money and Finance

The basics of budgeting, saving, and investing

I never learnt much about finances before graduating high school. I've regretted it ever since.

And I'm not alone.

Get smart about your money and let your money work for you. That way you'll end up with a lot more in the bank.

Below are some basic tips to make you less likely to end up broke and more likely to end up well-off. There are also some tips on how to handle it if you do go broke at some point.

The Three Golden Pots—How to Divvy Up Your Money Wisely

One pot (or jar—whatever term floats your boat) for immediate needs, such as food, rent, and insurance.

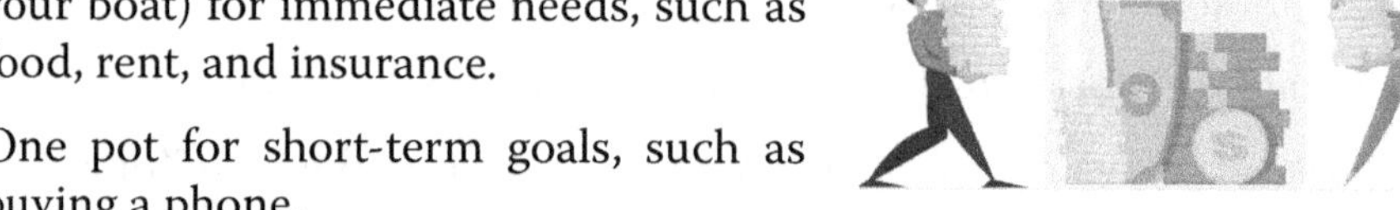

One pot for short-term goals, such as buying a phone.

One pot for long-term goals, such as traveling the world and saving for life after college and beyond.

That's the traditional approach to money management. You pop about one third of your earnings into each pot (possibly some extra into the immediate needs one, depending on how much money you earn). This approach teaches you to only spend what's in the first pot. If you have only one pot, you're much more likely to spend more, and when there's an emergency, or you want to go on vacation, there's no money to pay for it.

These days most people use bank accounts as "pots." Banks like Wise actually allow you to create these pots and name them instead of setting up different bank accounts. As for banks, check their fees and interest rates before you choose one, as well as what perks they offer. Newer banks and financial services tend to have very different perks from more old-fashioned banks. Some banks have special accounts for teens.

You could divide this into five pots instead.

One pot for immediate needs, such as rent, food, and insurance.

One pot for short-term goals, such as buying a phone.

One pot for emergencies, such as paying for a new laptop if the one you have breaks or going to the doctors when you have the flu.

One pot for long-term goals, like going to college, buying a home, and so forth. (This can be divided into two—shorter term goals like college and longer term goals like buying a home or moving overseas.)

One pot for savings you do not touch unless the roof falls down on your head (i.e. this is your retirement fund).

Some even add a sixth pot for charity—having money available for donations to good causes. Alternatively, they donate their time instead (which can be a lot more rewarding and fun in some instances, but as someone working with an NPO (non-profit organization), I also know how much cash donations are needed).

This kind of thinking will stop you from going on a spending spree every time you get paid. Because when you get paid, you immediately pay into your pots. You don't have a ton of money available. You only have enough to get you through the month.

If you want to buy something whenever you get paid (as a reward), choose something so small it won't affect your budget. Or buy something you'd need to buy anyway, such as a piece of clothing.

Now, the reality might be that with your income, you have to put 90% in the first pot. However, you have to consider that there will be emergencies. Things will never remain exactly the same—your phone, laptop, and washing machine will eventually break, and your car battery will need to be replaced. So no matter what you are earning right now, something needs to be saved. Otherwise, when the laptop crashes or when you need the dentist or whatever emergency it might be, you have nothing.

You need to learn to think about the future. If you have to eat noodles one day a week to save money, chances are you'll survive that. But if your pockets are empty next time you need a doctor, you might not survive that.

Do I sound harsh? I don't mean to scare you, but you do need money for emergencies, and it helps to pay for insurance.

Likewise, if you're used to using only organic food, you might be able to eat non-organic apples once a week if it helps you save $5 for a bag of apples.

Budgeting 101

While having three or five pots is great, you want to divide the first pot into different sections, so to speak.

You need to figure out what your living costs are and anything that does not go to living costs in this pot can either be used for entertainment or be put in the other pots.

1. Rent or mortgage and home maintenance
2. Food, toiletries, and cleaning supply
3. Bills like wifi and electricity (including things like buying data and airtime if you don't have a contract for your phone)
4. Any subscriptions and memberships (apps, software, gym membership, etc. and these are essentials, not your gaming apps—that's entertainment)
5. Insurance (and yes, you need it)
6. Maintenance of cars, bikes, etc. and fuel if needed and/or public transport

7. Clothes and shoes
8. Any other essentials (like haircuts, book supply for education, stationery, etc.)
9. Entertainment
10. Gifts (if you celebrate birthdays and the like)

Think before you buy a car that you will have to pay monthly payments for, or before you get a mortgage, or loan. Anything that ties you to pay for it over a period of time needs consideration. Try to save enough to have a really big down payment if you want to buy something like that.

On the flip side, if you need a car to get to work in another town, not having one might cost you *more* as you can't accept a good job offer.

Also, consider where you wish to live. In some places, living costs are a lot higher. Freelancers often work online so they can go live in places where they can keep their costs down. That way, they can save up and later choose where they want to live.

Expect the Unexpected—Budgeting for Life's Ups and Downs

When people say they are budgeting for starting a family, they often consider the essentials—food, insurance, extra costs at home, clothes, and education. That kind of thing.

But what if your kid turns out to have special needs or a medical condition? Needs therapy? Needs to see doctors regularly?

Or what if one of the parents loses their job and it takes six months to find a new one?

I'm not saying that *bad* things will happen. Maybe losing their job is the best thing that ever happened to that parent because they'll find a much better one. But they still don't have a salary for six months.

Maybe while you're at college, your older sister has a baby and the baby is a preemie and your sister needs you by her side for three months as her partner is away and the grandparents are unavailable or no longer with us. And she doesn't have money for a nanny. So you decide to pitch in. You might meet your next boyfriend or girlfriend while helping your sister or find your new boss, so what seems like an obstacle could turn out to be awesome. But you end up having to retake some modules the following term. And pay for them.

When you budget, expect the unexpected.

One way of tackling this is margins. If you expect to spend $100 on food this week, budget for $120 and put the extra in the savings pot by the end of the month if there's something left over. Or you can keep it in the "budget pot" so that you have extra for the coming months (for example, you might want to splurge during Christmas).

Before you set out on certain ventures, such as a trip around the globe, college, parenthood, setting up a business, or anything else, consider saving *more* than you need. That way, you're never short.

Remember to track what you have in your "pots" too.

Expenses (things you need to pay for)	Budget (the money you set aside for it)	Actual Expense (what you ended up paying)	Running Balance (what's left of your budget)
Rent			
Food			
Toiletries			
Bills			
Clothes			
Entertainment			
Subscriptions			

* This is a sample budget tracker, but you can create your own as long as it helps you keep track of your expenses and budget. There are lots of other templates and tools online if you want something more specific. Try filling up this sample tracker so you can get a feel of how it's done.

It's Only a Dollar—the True Cost of Small Expenses

"This new app looks fun. It's only $20 a month, so I'll get it. No big deal." In a year, that's $240. In ten years, $2,400. If you put that money in a bank account that offered interest, or invested it in something profitable, that would be even more in ten years' time.

"I like getting takeaway coffee in the morning when I go to work. It's only $5 and it's a treat that makes me feel positive about going to work." It's $25 per work week, $100 (and a bit) per month, $1,200 per year. In ten years, that's $11,200. Considering this, getting a takeaway coffee as a treat should perhaps be limited to one day per week.

The same consideration should go into choosing your next car, phone, or rental property—anything that requires monthly payments. What's "only" an extra $100 per month is $11,200 over 10 years. Some things are worth it, some aren't.

Always add things up.

And add up several things, too. You buy one takeaway coffee, one takeaway lunch, two chocolate bars, and one UberEats meal per week. What's the sum total of your small little treats that week?

It's similar to when we buy snacks. A bag of crisps here, a chocolate bar there, but at the end of the week, that's $10. Or $40 per month, which is $480 per year.

Also, consider what treats you're getting. For example, it doesn't cost the coffee company much more to make you a mocha than it does a latte, but what costs *you* more? Perhaps you stick to one mocha per week or only do mochas at home? You can buy a chocolate bar per week, but you bake cakes yourself as they cost too much to buy.

About that. The cakes, that is. While they may cost more than the chocolate bar, how much time does it take to bake it if you do it yourself?

Because if you're a freelancer working from home and losing time to baking, well, then you might need to buy the cake instead. On the flip side, you might get so bored always working from home that it's worth going to a coffee shop or co-working space twice a week. And if you find out you're three times more effective when working in a co-working space, then it's probably worth going there every day if it's affordable. Especially if you network with people who bring you new clients and contacts.

You also want to be smart about other things. What's the cost of a) driving your car to work, b) co-riding, or c) biking to work? Biking might be the cheapest, but it takes so much time you'd lose out on other things. Driving would be the fastest and most comfortable, but it's by far the most expensive (and bad for the environment). Co-riding is decently comfortable, fast, and economical. So in this case, it's the winner.

Save money where you can so you can afford to spend on the things that truly matter to you. And always weigh the benefits with the costs.

Let Your Money Work for You—Understanding Smart Investments

Robert Kiyosaki became famous because he taught people to buy houses to rent out, not to live in. By renting out a couple of houses and making an income, people could get enough money to buy their own house without being tied to their mortgage forever. Of course you need to know what you're doing if you decide to buy a house, though. If you buy a bad one, it will cost you more in repairs than it will bring in in rent, and you might end up having to sell at a loss if the housing market goes down and you need to recoup your investment.

Your money should be making you more money; it shouldn't disappear through your fingers like mist.

Some of the money in your long-term goals pot can be used for investments.

The first thing people will tell you about investments is that you should be able to lose the money and still be alright. Otherwise, don't invest it. Because investments come with risks.

This is why people tend to spread out their investments. Some in gold, some in the stock market, some in crypto, some in real estate, some in bonds, and some in companies.

Some people like short-term investments and do day trading. Other people invest their money in investments that are likely to pay off over time.

In the long run, the economy always fluctuates. It goes up. Then it goes down. People tend to be shocked when there's a crash in the market, but if things go too high, there invariably is a crash. What's more, the market can crash due to unexpected events, such as COVID-19. But if you look back over the centuries, there was the plague, the influenza, and so forth, so if you invest, you should know to expect the unexpected because it's expected!

If you can invest when the market is down and wait till it goes up to retrieve your investment, you make money.

If you invest when the market is on its way up and you keep your investments until it crashes, you lose money, unless you're able to retain your investments until the market goes up again. You also lose money if whatever you invested in disappears in the crash, such as a business you own shares in that goes bankrupt.

The best time to buy is, generally speaking, when the market is down and then hold on to your shares until it goes up and then sell them before it has a chance to go down again. But, as mentioned, sometimes it goes down unexpectedly.

That said, there's always money to be made—even when the market is down. When COVID-19 hit, the hand sanitizer and mask companies made a lot of money.

Even with services that people will always need (such as food), there are ups and downs in the market. After all, the price of potatoes one year is not the price of potatoes the next year. People's diets change. The availability of certain foods change—droughts, pest infestations, and the like are still present today.

Here are some basic guidelines for investing money:

- Invest only what you can afford to lose.
- Be realistic about what you can make from your investments—don't paint castles in the sky.
- Spread out (i.e. diversify) your investments. Invest them in different things that aren't all dependent on the same factors for being successful and perhaps do some high risk investments where you can earn more but lose it all and some low risk ones where you stand to earn less but are more stable and less likely to disappear on you.
- If you invest long-term, know that the market will fluctuate—go up and down (invest when it's down, get your money back when it's up).
- It is possible to make money in a recession.

- Learn as much as possible about what you want to invest in and get professional advice from different people (and not just the people who want your money) *before* you invest.
- Keep on top of your investments.
- If one investment goes well, don't fool yourself into thinking they all will. Keep a cool head and keep making strategic investments.
- Never ever invest in something if you don't know it's legit (and it's not legit just because your friend invested in it). And while on the topic, never hand out your credit card details unless you know an online store is 100% legit (and it can look legit even if it's not).

Also, learn to think outside the box. During the gold rush, more people became rich selling supplies to the miners than miners digging for gold.

Hitting Rock Bottom—Overcoming Financial Setbacks

A lot of people panic if they lose all their money, and trust me, it does happen. Perhaps it won't happen if you spent ten years diversifying your investments, but if it's your first year out of college and you lose your job, it's easy to hit rock bottom pretty fast.

If it happens, don't panic.

Immediately turn to people who can help you find a job—any job. Once you have *any* job, you can look for a *better* job. See the section below on earning an extra income for some ideas around jobs you can get that don't require lots of skill.

And if you know you can't pay your rent next month, instead of ending up on the street, immediately contact friends and family who can put you up or organizations that can help you. You can even couch surf using Couchsurfing.com or get a house sitting job or simply volunteer to do all the cleaning for a friend if they let you stay on their couch for one week in case you haven't gotten a job yet. Plan ahead, because when it's time to pay rent, you don't want to end up on the street.

Swallow your pride. Just because you lost money doesn't mean you lost the fabulous person that you are.

> Even if you took a detour and lost yourself for a while—becoming someone whom you are not proud of—consider that the real you is still inside you. You can still become that person.
>
> Even if you're 91.

And while on the topic of swallowing your pride, keep your dignity but don't try to keep up appearances. If you can save money by moving in with your family, do so. Take a few months to save up instead of getting into further debt by keeping your home. Sell the Porsche, buy an old Mini and paint it in psychedelic colors to cheer yourself up.

I'm joking.

Sort of.

I'd totally do that.

Only I'd buy a Beetle and paint it with flowers.

The point is, don't make yourself miserable thinking about what you've lost. Have fun with what you *have* and *can do* right now.

As someone who set out to live my dreams and followed them to the four corners of the world, I know all about couch surfing and living on a dollar (or five) a day. It's possible. I've done it.

I'm just here to tell you that when things go wrong, it's not the end of the road. You can reinvent yourself.

And when a door closes, a window opens. You have no idea what this new era of your life will bring. Keep your mind open to possibilities. If you sit sulking about what you've lost, you won't see the sign on the door where someone's looking to hire someone. A position that might make you richer than you've ever been.

Keep your eyes open for possibilities. Perhaps sleeping on your friend's couch for a week means you'll meet your next employer. You just never know. But when you have the right attitude, opportunities tend to present themselves.

Falling on hard times can be a convenient excuse for giving up, but it can also be an opportunity to rewrite your life and start a new chapter. And always remember the quote that decorates Shakespeare & Co. (a very special bookshop in Paris that houses writers for free), "Strangers are angels in disguise." You never know what your next meeting with someone will lead to. Your life can change in the blink of an eye. Even when you're at rock bottom, set your goals and have faith you'll reach them.

Earning an Extra Income

Even if you're doing well, if you earn a bit extra you can save more and do epic things like travel the world.

Earning a little extra can also come in handy when you have a job you love and which will take you places career-wise, but isn't paying well right now. Like starting out in the film industry, for example. What you can do to manage is get an extra job.

There are ways to make money online today that weren't available a few decades ago. Consider that you can work as a freelancer for just a few hours a week to top up your income. Platforms like Upwork make it easy to start out as a freelancer (though if you plan to make a career of it, it's great to keep your day job while you're setting up as it tends to take a while to build a client base).

Working weekends in a restaurant. Cleaning an elderly lady's house once a week. Working for a staffing agency that does catering for events. Babysitting. Helping out at a local store one day a week. If you have to, walk from door to door asking for work at businesses. Bring your résumé along and hand it to the manager. Even if they don't have any open positions right now, it can pay off down the line. These are also the kind of jobs you can look for if you end up losing your job and need something fast.

If you need funds for something specific, like surgery or to set up a business, then do a fundraiser. Platforms like GoFundMe can help you with that.

Look, there's always a way. Even if you have to sell cookies to the neighbors.

11

911–Preventing, Preparing for, and Handling Emergencies

A guide on how to handle common emergencies

Let's start with the most important thing here: attend a first aid course. Now. Immediately. When someone next chokes, you'll know what to do. When you get hurt, you'll know what to do.

In addition to that, let's look at some tips for preventing and handling emergencies.

Basic Safety Tips

Here are some tips for a safe home and safety in general:

- Unplug all devices before leaving home or going to bed.
- Unplug appliances like your toaster, hairdryer, or air fryer after using it—even if it's off.
- Set a timer when cooking so you don't forget something and it burns—and have a fire blanket or fire extinguisher in the kitchen as you cannot put out a fire with oil using water.
- Keep your phone charged at all times so that you can call people in case of an emergency.
- Plug in the numbers to local emergency services on your phone—some areas have special services, like mountain or sea rescue, snakebite first aid services, and so forth.

(155)

- Never leave candles near anything that could catch fire (and remember that a draft could move a curtain closer to a candle).
- Never leave candles on when you leave a room.
- Have a smoke alarm in almost every room.
- Have a fire extinguisher in several rooms.
- Have a checklist for what to turn off in your home before leaving the house and make sure to tick it off (you can put a whiteboard by the door).
- Carry a first aid kit with you.
- Carry water with you at all times, as well as a snack (you never know when you might get stuck—what if a car or bus breaks down somewhere?).
- If you live in an earthquake zone, pack an earthquake kit that you keep with you.
- Learn about particular dangers in your area (snakes, earthquakes, etc.) and how to deal with them.
- Always wear a helmet (when riding motorcycles) and seat belts. And NEVER text and drive or ride with someone who is doing this.

If something happens, take a deep breath. Keep your head cool. Sit down and put your head between your knees if you get dizzy. Keep breathing—slow breaths in through your nose and out through your mouth. You cannot deal with an emergency if you don't keep your head about you.

What to Do in Case of a Fire and How to Treat Burns

First of all, if you're on fire, stop, drop, and roll while covering your face.

Secondly, if the house is on fire, leave through the nearest exit, then call the emergency services or run to the nearest person who can do so. If you can't get out, immediately call for help. Heat rises, so stay close to the ground. Do not open windows unless that's where you plan to get out.

Opening a window can let more oxygen in the room, but oxygen will also fuel the fire. Do not touch metal without a blanket or similar to cover your hands as metal gets hot. If there's smoke, try to cover your mouth and nose. If you're by water, douse yourself in it.

Regular fires can be doused with water, but electrical fires require special fire extinguishers, sand, or a fire blanket. Likewise, when oil is on fire you need a fire blanket or fire extinguisher.

There's a lot more you can read up on about fire safety and what to do in case of a fire, so please do read up about it. Knowing what to do in a time of crisis is invaluable.

As for treating burns, burns are divided into different degrees of severity.

If you have a first-degree burn, you will experience redness and a bit of burning in the area. Exposure to hot water or spending too much time in the sun can cause this.

If a first-degree burn is only covering a small area, and after it gets better (stops burning), it stays better, you don't have to see a doctor *unless* it's a chemical burn (i.e. caused by a chemical).

If, on the other hand, a first-degree burn covers a larger area (such as having a bad sunburn all over your body) or it starts healing but gets worse again, see a doctor immediately. Small children also need medical attention even if it's just a first-degree burn that covers a relatively small area of the body.

To treat a first-degree burn, you can cool the area with water, then apply aloe vera. If it's an area that comes into contact with the clothes you're wearing, try wearing loose-fitting clothes. Also remove anything that might irritate the skin, such as jewelry. Be sure to drink plenty of fluids while healing.

Second-degree burns affect the first and second layers of the skin. If it's a small burn, you can treat it at home. If it covers a larger area (wider than about 2 inches or 5 centimeters) or swells quickly, you need to seek medical assistance. Likewise, if you've burned a sensitive area, such as your face or genitals, seek medical assistance right away. Any second-degree burn accompanied with smoke inhalation also requires medical attention right away.

Immediately cool the area in cold water for about ten minutes and apply aloe vera or cocoa butter afterwards. If you burned your mouth, put a piece of ice in your mouth. Be sure to remove anything tight around the affected area as soon as possible (before it swells up). Do not pop blisters—they help protect the skin. Loosely bandage the burn with a clean bandage and take a painkiller if needed.

If you suspect a burn isn't healing as it should, seek medical assistance immediately.

Third-degree burns are burns that affect all three layers of the skin. For this, you always need a doctor no matter how small the affected area is. The affected area might appear charred, look dry and leathery, or have patches of white, brown, or black.

Do not try to treat third-degree burns by yourself, do not remove burned clothing that's stuck to the skin, and do not run cold water over them—simply leave them. If something, like jewelry, or clothing not sticking to the skin can be removed, do so. The area can swell, and it might be hard to get it off later. Loosely (really loosely) wrap the area with clean gauze or a clean cotton sheet if the area is large (never use anything that is fluffy and can stick to the skin). If it's another person who's been affected, keep an eye on their pulse and breathing. If needed, perform CPR. If you're the one affected, call for help right away. If it's a larger area that's been burned or you have inhaled smoke, call emergency services.

If just one body part is affected, try to keep it above the heart, such as raising an arm or laying someone on the floor (if they do not have a back, neck, or head injury) and raising their leg up. Laying someone on the floor and propping their legs up can also help prevent shock (you can raise their legs by about 12 inches or 30 centimeters. Do not place a pillow under their head if there's an airway burn as it can prevent breathing.

Do not try to blow on a third-degree burn, nor apply water or any form of ointment. Try to not cough, sneeze, or breathe on it, too.

If someone is on fire, tell them to stop, drop, and roll on the ground. Get something to wrap them in immediately to put out any lingering fire and pour water on top. Then seek medical assistance right away.

You should seek medical attention if:

- A burn, even mild, covers a large area of your body
- A child has been burned
- It's a second-degree burn that affects an area that's wider than about 2 inches or 5 centimeters, or an area that's a sensitive part of your body (face, groin, nipple, ear, etc.)
- The affected area swells quickly

- It's a third-degree burn (of any size)
- The area appears charred, dry and leathery, or have brown, white, or black spots
- It's accompanied by a fever, chill, or other signs of distress
- It's a chemical burn (any size)
- It's a burn caused by lightning
- There has been smoke inhalation
- The person goes into shock
- The burn is due to physical abuse

If it's a first- or second-degree burn:

- Cool the area with water
- Remove any tight-fitting clothing, jewelry, or other items touching the skin
- Apply aloe vera
- Loosely wrap it with a clean bandage
- If it covers a larger area, depending on the size, immediately call for an ambulance or go to the hospital after first cooling it down and dressing it
- Do NOT remove blisters

If it's a third-degree burn:

- If someone is on fire, tell them to stop, drop, and roll while you find a blanket, rug, or anything to roll them in and pour water over them
- If it's a *chemical* burn, remove the substance while protecting yourself and rinse the affected area with water (granted the substance can be removed with water). Do NOT apply water on other third-degree burns
- Call an ambulance
- Ensure the person is breathing and their pulse is stable—apply CPR if needed
- Remove any clothing or jewelry that does not stick to the skin of the affected area (if it sticks to the skin, do not touch it)
- Wrap them in a loose gauze or clean sheet (nothing fluffy, not even fleece)

- Place any burned body part above heart level if possible
- Put them flat on their back and raise their legs 12 inches or 30 centimeters to prevent shock (only if their back or airways are not burnt and they do not have any back, neck, or head injuries)

Treating Falls and Other Impact Injuries

If someone has fallen or had some form of impact collision, do not move them until you ascertain there is no head, neck, or back injury. If you suspect there might be, call an ambulance. Try to keep them and their head still—put something down that prevents them from moving—especially their head.

If you see a person is not breathing, apply CPR.

If someone appears to have hurt a limb, apply ice. If you suspect something might be broken or out of alignment, see a doctor immediately.

If someone appears fine, but afterwards is dizzy, disorientated, fuzzy, or has issues walking, seek medical attention.

Treating Cuts and Wounds

If it's a *small* wound, disinfect it with a disinfectant if you have one, water if you don't, then put on some antibiotic ointment or petroleum jelly over the wound, and use a bandage to cover it. If it bleeds a lot at the start, put some pressure on it with something clean before you wash it and put on the bandage, or simply wrap it up with a bandage.

Change the dressing and clean the wound once a day. Note that some wounds heal faster when exposed to air, so once it starts to heal, try to get rid of the bandage.

If the wound is in a place where it's hard not to, so to speak, crack it open when you move about, check with a pharmacist what to do. You might get rubbing alcohol to help dry the wound while it's healing, or you might need to always keep a Band-Aid on apart from when you sit still for a while and air the wound.

If someone is bleeding profusely, the first thing you want to do is to staunch the blood flow. Apply pressure with a clean cloth or gauze. Do not remove it to check if the wound has stopped bleeding, as that can set it off again. If the cloth gets soaked through, apply another without removing the first.

Try to keep the bleeding body part as high as possible. If it's their arm, have them raise it above their head. If it's their leg, lie them down and place the leg on a chair (granted they have not sustained a head, neck, or back injury).

If it's a wound on their feet, arms, or legs, you can cut off the blood supply a bit by tying something around their arm or leg closer to the body than the injury (so if the injury is on the ankle, you can cut off the blood supply a bit by tying something around the thigh). There are also special pressure points on the body to help cut off blood supply to some body parts—you can look these up or take a first aid course to learn more.

You can furthermore apply ice to the area to make the blood vessels contract and prevent swelling.

Note that head wounds, even minor ones, bleed a lot even if they aren't, so to speak, dangerous.

Any larger cuts and wounds (deep or long ones) should be seen by a doctor as they may need stitching or some other form of care that you might not be able to provide.

Any wounds that are dirty, have been caused by animals, or are deep might require a tetanus shot, so see a doctor.

Hopefully, this chapter has taught you a thing or two about handling various emergencies. But—and that should be a huge BUT—sign up for a first aid course as soon as possible.

It can help you save lives, your own included.

This guide is nowhere near as helpful as attending an actual course.

Why? Because when you do a course, you act things out. And by acting them out, you learn. So that when something happens, you know how to carry out whatever help is needed. What's more, right now you know, theoretically speaking, what first-, second-, and third-degree burns are, but what do they look like? Seeing real-world images and acting out what to do in case it happens is the best way to prepare yourself for if and when it does happen.

If you don't have the money to attend a course, check YouTube to find whatever you can online. And don't just watch things—practice them. Decide to watch an online first aid course with a friend and practice with each other. By doing, you learn. And you remember.

Another tip is to meditate and do breathing exercises regularly, because when there's an emergency, you need to keep your head cool and mindfulness exercises have proven beneficial when it comes to that.

PART 5
PERSONAL DEVELOPMENT

12

Charting Your Path

Tips for career planning

No one can tell you what the perfect career is—you have to make that choice.

What you can do, however, is figure out a few things that might help you make the choice.

Consider What You Enjoy

If you love math and are good at it, look into careers where you get to do math. The same goes for anything you love doing and are good at that is related to a career path (and pretty much anything is!).

In short, figure out what you enjoy and research career paths where you get to do things relating to that.

Consider What Your Personality Is Like

You can change. Of course you can. But if you don't enjoy confrontation and know you would loathe to spend all day arguing people's cases, then becoming a defense attorney is likely not the right choice for you.

If you don't like working under pressure, then the ER or a professional kitchen are probably not your future workplaces. If, on the other hand, you love a good challenge and work like a dream under pressure, then these are workplaces where you'd thrive.

If you're brilliant with people, consider jobs where you get to interact with people.

Simply write down some personality traits you have, or just bear them in mind, and then return to the list of career paths that encompass things you enjoy doing and also see if some options would work well with your personality. For example, if you love math, you might have listed becoming a math professor as one option. But if you don't enjoy spending time interacting with a lot of people, teaching students would be difficult. If you're just shy or feel insecure presenting things in front of a group, you can overcome it by attending workshops that teach people skills and presentation techniques, but if you genuinely prefer to be alone, you might want to consider another career path.

Consider What Your Values Are

We all have values. Some of us value honesty, others value playfulness, inventiveness, kindness . . . the list goes on. Check your list and see if you can find a career path where you not only get to do something you love, are good at, and that matches your personality but also ties into your values.

For example, while working for a big ad agency might be creative, challenging, and allows you to work with people, if the ad agency takes on clients like cigarette companies or companies that aren't environmentally friendly, would you still be happy working for them?

This is something you want to remember when applying for work, too. Does the company you're applying for have similar values to your own?

Consider the Day-to-Day Life a Certain Career Will Bring You

Being an actress might sound glamorous. Going to hundreds of auditions to get one job while simultaneously working as a waitress might not sound as glamorous. Neither, perhaps, is showing up at five a.m. on set once you get the job and hanging about until nine when they start shooting your scene. Consider the day-to-day life you'd have if you choose a certain career path.

Talk to people in your chosen industry. Do summer internships. Learn. Figure out if it's for you.

Consider Your Industry

Are there many jobs in the fields you're looking at? Is that about to change any time soon? What's the salary like? What's your growth potential (i.e. can you start chopping vegetables and end as head chef)? What are disruptors that might, well, disrupt this industry (such as AI)?

Figure out if what you learn about your industry aligns with your career goals—if you want to get rich within ten years, becoming a waitress likely isn't the way to go. Then again, there's always the exception—become a waitress and buy the place you're working at. Anything is possible, but for this exercise, it helps to check out what is likely to happen if you walk a certain path.

Map Your Career Path

Is higher education necessary for what you want to do? If not, would it still be nice to get a degree because you'll learn how to think differently about various subjects?

Education isn't all about getting somewhere in your career, but also how you approach life *and* any future job. You might not need film school to become a director, but it can help you become a *better* director.

Nor is it all about higher education. These days, there are a ton of online classes—including ones from universities like Yale. You can continue to learn and grow, whether you go to college or not. And if you do go to college, you can continue to grow with masterclasses online once you leave.

Another important thing to remember is that sometimes soft skills are as valuable as technical skills in your particular field. For example, a dentist will likely do much better in their practice if they have good people skills, as people won't use their services unless they feel comfortable. Even great dentists lose clients if they're awkward in interactions.

At other times, it's about complementary skills. No, you don't need to learn accounting or marketing to become a plumber, but if you want to run your own plumbing business, those two skills might be the difference between whether you run a successful business or not.

So when you map out what educational path to take, also consider the additional skills you'll need to be successful in your chosen profession.

When you decide whether to pursue higher education (or any education) you have to balance cost necessity for your career path, improved value to what you can offer, improved value to your life (because education isn't just about your profession), and time.

The next chapter on self-reliance might help you further in deciding what career to pursue and whether or not to attend higher education.

It's not just education you need to consider, but how to navigate your career path once you start working. There are regular and irregular career paths. You can train as a chef, start a blog, become an influencer, and cater events. That's less straightforward than working your way up in a restaurant.

Consider your options. Brainstorm. Read up on what influencers in that field have to say.

If you chose a certain career, map out what you have to do to get to where you want to be. What's the best, most enjoyable, and fastest route to get there? Be practical, but also listen to your intuition and, as just mentioned: think outside the box. Sit for a few minutes with your eyes closed, taking slow breaths, and asking yourself what path to take. Because sometimes, the most logical route is not the best one for you.

13

Becoming Self-Reliant and Independent

Tips and strategies for developing autonomy and independence (goals, questioning beliefs, becoming self-referential)

Below you'll find some tips for living a charmed life . . . or simply living *your* best life.

Changing Patterns and Setting Goals (and Achieving Them!)

We all have patterns in life—whether always being on time, fumbling when nervous, spending too much money, being too tight with money, or binge-watching Netflix when stressed. Some patterns are useful, others not so much.

If you want to change a pattern (habit) in your life or achieve a goal, there are some things that can help you.

If it's something practical, such as achieving something tangible (such as breaking a pattern of eating unhealthy foods or becoming a doctor), you can break your goal into achievable steps. Further down, in the part about Changing Your Actions and Reactions—Shaping Habits, we'll talk more about breaking patterns and also discuss less tangible things, such as staying calm under pressure or being on time.

First, break your goal into small steps that are easy to take. Remember what we did in the chapter about diet?

If not, here's a reminder: don't try to go from eating only junk food to eating only healthy foods overnight unless it's crucial you do so. Start by cutting down on soda—switch to raw fruit juice. Then switch to half fruit juice and half water. Then tackle your snacks, then your breakfasts, then your lunches, then your dinners, then your desserts.

If it has to do with exercise, don't go from not running at all to running for an hour seven days a week. Start with five minutes walking, five minutes running every day for the first week. The second week, you do seven minutes running, five minutes walking. The third week, you do ten minutes running, five minutes walking. And so forth.

Perhaps you're happy to start with ten minutes running, five minutes walking the first week and jump to fifteen minutes running and five minutes walking the next week. Great. You set the pace. Just don't push yourself so hard that you end up dropping out somewhere along the way as it's too hard.

Besides, do you have to run seven days a week? Probably not. After all, your body needs to recover.

Remember the 80/20 rule. In short, don't try to go from zero to hero. If you want to change a habit, make it easy—break it down in chunks and tackle one thing per week. There are fifty-two weeks in a year. By the end of the year, you can change fifty-two things. If you try to change everything the first week, on the other hand, chances are you'll fall off the bandwagon and have to start all over again the next year, or month, or what have you.

Secondly, find people who want to achieve the same thing or change the same habit. Having people whom you can bond with over it will help you stick it out.

Likewise, having someone keeping you accountable will help. Perhaps have a friend or relative check in by the end of each day if you achieved your goals that day.

Lastly, sit down by the end of each day and write down what you did in relation to your goal or changing your habit. Pat yourself on the back. And every so often, celebrate. Vary how you celebrate or reward yourself and vary when you do it. But give yourself those things from time to time.

Why do I say to vary it?

Because the rewards system in your brain works better if it isn't always the same reward and you aren't rewarded *every* time you do something good.

Another way to help ensure you nail your goals is to turn them into SMART goals.

Specific
Measurable
Achievable
Relevant
Timed

You want to become a doctor by a certain year (that's specific, measurable, achievable . . . in the long run, and timed, and it's relevant because it's a dream that makes your heart sing).

This year, to achieve your goal, you have to get an A in biology and chemistry and a B in math to get into your chosen college (specific, timed, and measurable, as well as relevant to your goal).

To achieve the grades you want, this week you have to do A, B, C (such as spending fifteen minutes a day studying each subject, on Wednesday practicing for two hours for a test, on Thursday asking your teacher any questions you have after studying, studying for another hour, then getting an A on the test on Friday). Write your weekly goals (or tasks) down in your diary. Tick them off when you complete them. And smile at yourself for being great.

Here you can see how a long-term goal can be broken down into achievable chunks. While becoming a doctor of medicine is achievable, it's not achievable right now. And for a goal to be smart, you need to be able to break it down into achievable mini goals.

Understanding What You Truly Want and Being Realistic About It

You want to become a ballet dancer. You dance once a week. You like it. Right.

But what's the life of a ballerina like?

You dance two hours a day, in addition to other types of training and rehearsals. Your feet bleed and become malformed. Your salary expectations are fairly low. The length of your career is short. You likely have to teach in addition to get roles where you perform. Potential downsides healthwise are injuries and the need for surgery, such as hip replacement, when you get older.

You close your eyes. You imagine the life of a ballerina. What your body feels like. What the food you eat tastes like. How many times you have to practice a piece to get it right. What your feet feel like at the end of the day. What it's like to audition for pieces and be turned down. What it's like to get a role. What it's like to work with other dancers. What it's like being on stage. How you will feel at the beginning and end of your career.

Why am I on about all of this?

Because being a ballerina isn't all about performing a piece on stage. The day-to-day life is so much more.

Just like being an actor isn't all about being famous. In fact, you might never become famous. Do you still want to act? Do you want to be on set at five a.m and stay till eleven p.m.? Do you want to perform six days a week in the West End or on Broadway? Are you willing to have other jobs while you work your way up the ladder? What would those jobs be?

Being a doctor isn't all about saving lives. It's also about losing patients you can't save. Grueling exams before you even become a doctor. Having to perform autopsies. Seeing patients in pain. Seeing happy patients whom you help cure.

You need to enjoy the day-to-day life of the profession you choose. Not just some glorious dream of that one moment the profession might bring you.

Look, no dream is impossible, but get realistic about how to achieve it and what life will be like once you achieve it.

Being realistic will also help you in convincing your parents or future college board that you truly want to do something.

"I'm off to Hollywood to become an actress after drama school, Mom." Right. So how will you survive while auditioning? If you don't like bartending, that can be an issue. Figure out the way to survive that you would LOVE and that also brings you closer to your goal should you not land a role on day one (though you might).

I've lived in Hollywood and I loved it because I was happy to be in LA and I love film, but some people were desperately unhappy because they weren't famous. If they wanted to become famous, perhaps becoming an influencer would have been easier. If they wanted to act, perhaps getting a job in a theater troupe would have been easier. There's no saying they couldn't still work their way to LA, but it would help them *enjoy* their lives while doing so!

It's the same if you want to go to college and need to work to pay for tuition. Being in college won't be fun if you have to work jobs you absolutely hate, so plan ahead. What job would you like? What would bring you joy? Can you do an internship now that will help you land a job later?

Intuition and Goal Setting

Look, some people will tell you that intuition is poppycock. Nonsense. Doesn't exist.

I beg to differ.

I leave it to you to decide whether it's a real thing or not, but I will share what I think can be helpful when it comes to using your intuition—that thing that goes beyond your rational mind and your ego or perhaps uses your rational mind in ways you can't explain.

You see, when it comes to goals, it's all very well to know *what* you want, but is that want driven by the ego or the heart?

Close your eyes and think about it. Feel into it when you next meditate.

When you look at things *realistically* and *intuitively* you will discover that all that glitters isn't gold.

For example, you want to be a lawyer fighting for human rights because you love people. And you heard that Amal Clooney did some good things and she's really cool. And famous. And has a fab wardrobe. You imagine yourself at big conferences for the UN, delivering keynote speeches. Traveling the world, solving problems. Your name in the newspapers.

Right.

Is your desire to become a lawyer driven by your ego or your heart? And would those things you dream about really make you happy? Or would actually caring for people (as opposed to spending all your time doing paperwork so as to argue a case) make you happier?

> Check what it is your heart wants and not just what your mind thinks is the right thing to do for one reason or another.

Likewise, when you set goals to achieve things, consider that the most logical way of getting what you want isn't always the best way. Close your eyes and ask yourself what you need to do to achieve the goals you have this week or today. Tune in to them.

Let's say you need to study for a biology test tomorrow. You close your eyes and ask yourself what you need to do to be successful in this. You get a feeling you should go with your friend, Lindsey, after school and study at her place (which seems *illogical* because usually you study better alone). Still, you follow your intuition and go to her place, and while you study together, her older brother, who majors in biology, comes home and offers to help you with your test.

Intuition is different from a want. If you want to go to Lindsey because you don't really want to study, then you're driven by a need for pleasure instead of intuition. It's the same when you want to get up and have some candy instead of reading your book. That's not your intuition speaking. And you'll have to learn to see (or, rather, feel) the difference between the two.

Intuition often goes against logic. For example, you might suddenly get a feeling that you should drive the long way to work. Logically, it makes no sense. But when you later find out that if you'd gone the short way, you would have been stuck in traffic because there was an accident, you understand that it was, in fact, logical to go the long way. The problem is that often we overrule logic with reason and other times we think that our "desires" are our intuition speaking. It takes some practice to learn to slow down and feel into things and learn to decipher our feelings.

There is an excellent book by a neurosurgeon called *Into the Magic Shop* that talks about how to distinguish between the ego and the heart. It's a fascinating account of man's journey of "getting what he wants." It's also an incredibly inspirational story. And the surgeon and author's name is James Doty. In case you were wondering.

Setting Goals That Make You Happy

You want to become an entrepreneur. In the field of physics. You have some ideas. You know you want to get a major in physics and a minor in business. And you're going to set up a small business already now, just to figure out how to do the books. Get an understanding of how to make money.

Fabulous.

Or perhaps, you want to continue working alongside the gardener you already help out and eventually build up your own clientele and start your business. Just take a course in business management (basic accounting, marketing, and the likes) along the way.

Wonderful.

But how do you want to feel while you're working toward becoming an entrepreneur? And how do you want to feel once you become an entrepreneur? What do you want your *day-to-day life* to look like? Do you get up at five, go for a run while listening to a book related to your field, then have a power breakfast while hurrying off to work, after which you are a super ninja at work, then come home late and hit the sack? Or are you a nine-to-fiver who works a little bit on a Saturday and then goes fishing for the weekend? What do you do at night? Who are your friends? What hobbies do you pursue, if any? What personality traits are you building? What's your attitude like?

Goals aren't just about that one thing we want to achieve—they are also about the things that make us happy. You can have a goal to do salsa one day a week. You can have a goal to make more friends. You can have a goal to show up being more outgoing or open-minded. You can have a goal to laugh more and, therefore, need to figure out the things you need to do for this to happen.

Goals aren't just about the big stuff you want to achieve. You should have a goal to create a day-to-day life that you enjoy. And if one area of your life isn't working—if you find it hard to create friendships, for example—you should have a goal to improve that area. You have to figure out how to do that. In this example, do you need to read books about people skills and how to create great relationships? Do you need to attend more social events? Do you need to work on your self-esteem?

While it might seem like a cool goal to earn enough money to drive a Porsche, how will achieving that make you feel? What will it add to your life?

The bottom line? Create goals that aim to make you happy and fulfilled.

The Importance of Daily Intentions

Setting intentions might sound like some fluffy New Age thing, but it's actually really helpful if you want to show up as your best self and have an epic time no matter what it is you're doing.

When you go into a meeting, what's your so-called intention? Purpose? What do you want out of the meeting?

Do you want to:

- Do your best
- Be of service
- Be open-minded but skeptical (see Don Miguel's epic five agreements for more on this and doing your best)
- Avoid making snap decisions or assumptions and leave your biases by the doorstep (decisions and assumptions are usually made based on biases)

If you say yes to the above, you end up being pretty present in the moment, taking in what's going on instead of what your biases would like you to *think* is going on. What's more, it opens you up to the people in the room as you wish to show up as your best self and serve in whatever way you can.

Instead of, say, trying to impress the interviewer in a predetermined way that might not at all help you, the interviewer might, in fact, not be open to that kind of approach. For example, you might have decided to be super confident and outgoing, but the interviewer turns out to be timid and gets intimidated by your approach. By being present, you take in what's happening, are able to course-correct, and can offer up your best self in any situation.

Those are goals for *any* interaction, by the way. If you just bear those four things in mind, you'll do pretty well in most situations.

You also need to have your own personal intentions.

If your meeting is a job interview, your goal might be to a) establish if the job is a fit for your skills, personality, and values and b) get the interviewer to see that you are a fit, if indeed you are.

Or it could be that you know this is the job you've been looking for and your intention is to show you've got the skills and personality required for it.

Whatever you're doing, whether meeting friends for dinner, doing a test, or driving somewhere, you can have an intention. If you're driving to work, you want to enjoy a relaxed ride and arrive safely. If you're spending time with friends or family, it might be to be present, or get to know them better, or create a memorable experience of some kind.

Having intentions help us keep on track. For example, if you want to enjoy a relaxed ride and arrive safely when driving to work, it might not be the right choice to take the route that's five minutes faster, without scenic views, and with a lot of aggressive drivers. Even if it would get you to work faster. The route is more likely to make you stressed, and you're more likely to have an accident as the drivers on that route are more aggressive.

Before you do anything, stop for a moment, close your eyes, and ask yourself: what do I want out of this? What is my intention?

Then, with your eyes still closed, ask yourself what you need to do to achieve it. What actions do you need to take? Sometimes your intuition might serve up something around this.

Remember as well that whenever you interact with people, there's a chance they'll act out. They've had a bad day. They're tired. You remind them of someone they dislike. They get jealous of you. Referring back to the previous example about the job interview, there's a myriad of reasons why the person doing the job interview isn't nice.

Don't react. Don't make a snap decision that this person is a moron and use that as an excuse to be rude.

What's your intention? If it's to get the job, then act accordingly—the interviewer might be a genuinely disagreeable person, but that doesn't need to get in your way of obtaining the job!

Besides, whenever someone reacts unfavorably to you, remember that what they're reacting to is likely not you. Not really. They are reacting to something inside themselves. Some stuff they have going on.

Even if the person offers up some constructive feedback that hits the nail on the head (whether the feedback is handed out in a nice or nasty manner), do you have to feel bad about it?

No.

So that horrible job interviewer just pointed out one of your worst traits in a nasty way. You feel hurt and, because of that, you feel angry.

Do you have to feel that way?

No.

You are a fantastic person at your core, even if you have an issue being on time, controlling your temper, sticking with your goals . . . whatever it is.

Acknowledge the feedback. Act on the feedback, if beneficial. But don't belittle yourself in the process or lash out at the person giving you the feedback.

In short, master yourself in the situation by referring back to what your intention for the interaction is.

Let's take another example. Let's say you're going to have a date at home with your partner and the power goes off just after you burn the food . . . what do you do? Let's say your intention, or end result if you so like, is to have a date with your partner where you connect deeply. Can you do that while eating a takeaway sitting by a candlelit table?

Sure you can.

It's not the date you *planned* (i.e. an excellent home-cooked meal), but you can still connect deeply with your partner.

Don't let circumstances or people's behavior stop you from achieving your intention and end result. Or, phrased differently, react in relation to your intention, not just the situation.

Changing Your Actions and Reactions— Shaping Habits

You are trying to study a certain subject for an hour a day, in addition to attending classes, and studying extra for tests as you've fallen behind. It's not your favorite subject, so you find it hard to concentrate.

As a result, when you get home, everything else appears more interesting than sitting down to study, so it's hard for you to do it. Instead, most days you find yourself taking a break to eat, then going on social media, having a shower . . . anything to distract yourself from studying.

There are things you can do to break the habit. The first thing you can do to make this easier is to decide you will study for only ten minutes, then take a break.

Anyone can do that, right?

Or not.

You're still distracted even if you know you just have to do it for ten minutes.

So you go into another room where there is no television, no clothes you can put away, no phone you can play on, no people you can look at. No distractions. Then you do the ten minutes before taking a five-minute break. Then you go back for another ten minutes. And so on until you reach sixty minutes worth of studying. You might even find that you can do twenty or thirty minutes at a time pretty quickly. The trick is to think it's only ten minutes as it won't bring up as much resistance. As mentioned, we can endure most things for ten minutes.

Also, enlist a friend to call you to check if you've done the studying every night. That will keep you accountable. Even just writing it down in your diary and ticking it off can help keep you accountable.

And remember to reward yourself when you get your work done. At least sometimes.

All these techniques were mentioned earlier in the chapter, but it sometimes helps to repeat some things!

Here's another tactic for changing your life that was mentioned in an earlier chapter—rethinking your life.

Every morning, sit down and think about how you wish the day to unfold. Think especially hard on certain things you wish to achieve. For example, if you want to remain calm during an exam, imagine the exam and how you will feel—first the nerves, and then the calm settling in as you look through the paper and start writing. If a question rattles you as you don't know the answer—or think you don't—you calmly move on to the next question and in the end, come back to the one you're unsure about. You imagine finishing all the questions you know first, then tackling the rest while reminding yourself that if you don't pass this test, there will be another. You will be fine. And you will do as well as you possibly can on this test.

Basically, you think through what you want to happen and your reactions. If you suspect there might be upheaval (like having to endure a board meeting with a bunch of people who love to scream and shout), imagine the best possible outcome in that upheaval and how you will react in the circumstances and steer the meeting to where you want to take it.

Then, at the end of the day, think through how the day actually unfolded. If you did something you didn't want to do or reacted in a way you didn't want to react, rethink it. Think about how you wish it would have unfolded.

For example, you had to give a presentation and it didn't go very well. Rethink it as you wish it would have happened.

By doing this, you retrain your brain.

I used the example of a test, presentation, and board meeting, but you can do this to rethink your inability to concentrate. Instead of imagining coming home and getting distracted when you're going to study, imagine what it feels like when your brain switches on and you concentrate. Then imagine how good it will feel when you complete the task. Keep imagining this until it becomes second nature to concentrate.

Mastering Time Management

Here are some questions you need to ask yourself if you're going to master time management.

What *must* get done today?

> Do this first.

What would be good to get done today?

> Do this if you have the time.

What actions do I need to take today to reach my long-term goals?

> Allocate time daily or weekly for this so it does not end up getting lost in the daily flurry of events.

What should I do today to feel good about myself?

Meditate, breathe, spend time outside, exercise—if you do this upon awakening, know that no matter what, you achieved something today.

What can I do today to enjoy myself?

This may or may not fit into a super hectic day, but chances are if you love to draw, read, cook, chat with your best friend, or just watch the clouds go by, you can fit in ten minutes a day for this even on a hectic day.

What can I do to relax for at least half an hour at the end of the day?

This could be something you enjoy or something that makes you feel good about yourself, as mentioned above, but it could also be something else, such as reading a book.

Time management experts such as Kevin Kruse also suggest that you:

1. Allocate time in your diary for each task and ensure that you stick to the time you have to perform it.
2. Start by doing your most important tasks first as that's when you have the most energy.
3. Leave the office by the time you're spent—after a certain hour, you become inefficient and it's a waste of time to work then.
4. Only check messages, emails, and do phone calls at certain allocated times every day.

EXERCISE

Get your calendar or planner out and start filling out what you need to do in the coming week.

Becoming Self-Referential

One thing with becoming an adult is that you are at a liberty to decide based on your own thoughts and values. Your parents can no longer tell you what you *should* think and *should* do.

The issue? You often find that when it's up to you to make the decisions, you have no idea what to think about things and what actions to take!

If someone came to you with an outrageous idea, such as the world being round, when clearly you can see that it's flat, you have to decide whether to:

1. Take their word for it without questioning it—after all, they sound knowledgeable.
2. Denounce them without questioning it—after all, everyone in the village says sit's flat.
3. Ask them to explain and demonstrate their theory to you in such a way that you can grasp it. Then ask some other highly educated individuals in the field whether or not they agree and why. What are they basing their assumptions on? Perhaps even read a book on the topic and try to understand it for yourself.

When we are young, we tend to take people's word for things. Dad said the conservative party is right, so they are right. Mom said the liberal party is right, so they are right. Then we reach a certain age and realize both Mom and Dad can't be right. So what's the truth?

Whenever something is presented to you, you have to ask yourself:

1. Is this presented by someone who is biased or not?
2. Is this presented by someone who knows what they are talking about or not?
3. Do other people who understand this particular topic agree or disagree?
4. What can I learn about this topic myself?
5. How biased am I?

To blindly accept other people's opinions is usually not a great idea. Question everything you learn. Question why things are done the way they are. But don't pretend you know how they should or shouldn't be done unless you've studied the topic.

If it's something to do with personal decisions, in addition to seeking knowledge, sit down and close your eyes. Meditate. Ask yourself to let go of any thoughts and feelings you have around something. Then ask yourself what you really think and want.

You have to become self-referential. You cannot rely on your friends, partner, family, or anyone else to guide you—you can listen to people's thoughts about something if they are knowledgeable, but you still have to make the final decision.

Some people are incredibly charismatic and seem so nice and kind. What's more, they seem authoritative. They appear to know what they're talking about. But do they? And are they the *only* ones knowledgeable on that topic? Ask around. Don't be misled by a smoothtalker.

With the Internet, a lot of fake news has been spread around. And by the way, many unethical people call authentic news fake news in order to discredit the truth for their own gain. You have to *question* the sources of what you read. Look for credible, authoritative sources.

On the flip side, there will be times you have to question authority.

Just because things are a certain way and people in authority want to keep them that way doesn't mean it's the right way.

For example, old practitioners of a trade often stick to practicing that trade the way they were taught, even though newer and better methods have been developed since.

When it comes to medicine, it can be downright dangerous.

It's just as dangerous to follow the latest fad just because you heard from a celebrity that they cured themselves of an ailment that way.

On the other hand, what they did could actually work.

So what do you do?

You try it. Under the guidance of a doctor. There is more and more research around herbal medicine as well as thinking yourself well. But the people who are serious about those approaches always suggest you try them while supervised by a medical professional. For example, I used Dr. John Sarno's method to cure repetitive strain injury after I failed using every conventional approach. Dr. John Sarno worked for New York University and advised everyone to get a diagnosis before using his approach. Ironically, I had disregarded his work because surely I couldn't *think* a physical problem away. But I did.

But I'm not a doctor. And you shouldn't take my advice on this as I am just sharing my experience. You should hear it, then do your own research and consult specialists.

What I'm trying to say is that you should have an open mind but use caution and reason when exploring new approaches to just about anything. How you were trained to think isn't necessarily right. But jumping ship without guidance might lead you to sink.

If you read Noah Yuval Harari's *Sapiens: A Brief History of Humankind*, you'll come to see that society, throughout the ages, has varied greatly. Yet, in each age, they were convinced that how they lived was *the* way to live. And if you look at any country today, some people in each country tend to think how they live is the right way to live. Then they point fingers at people living in other countries saying how they live is the wrong way to live.

It's not necessarily the wrong way, it's just a different way.

You have to find your way to live.

Go out there. Question. Learn. Have fun. Enjoy every little bit of life that you can!

In Closing

I hope this book has opened your eyes and helped you see that you can live a great life.

I hope it will help you manage yourself and your life, relationships, household, and finances better.

I also hope you will question what I've taught you in this book—try it out, but be skeptical. Learn more. Because, honestly, there is no user's guide to life.

Unfortunately.

A bit of a hiccup in the system there.

There are, on the other hand, a lot of clever people who have studied things like emotions, self-esteem, habits, goal setting, relationships, finances, household management, and cooking and learned things that could change your life. Drastically.

This book is, hopefully, a stepping point, something you can use to get further than where you are and then find other resources that can take you further. And remember—even this book can be overwhelming, so tackle one thing at a time. You don't have to learn about body language and mood boosters at *the same time*. Read the entire book in one go if you like, but then master one or two things at a time.

And here's the deal: you have to practice what you learn in this book to *actually* change any area of your life. So tackle one exercise at a time. Go out there and try them out.

Learn, explore, and have fun. If you fall over, laugh. Yeah, it hurts, but everyone falls. Find the humor. Find the learnings. Find the beauty that is beyond whatever pain the fall causes. Because there will be something there once you get up again. Even if, right now, it feels like you'll be stuck in a mud heap forever. But you won't.

When you aren't lying in the mud because you just toppled over, appreciate what life has to offer. There's so much to enjoy.

Really.

So go enjoy it!